I0820092

GATHER TOGETHER

Delightful Décor & Simple Recipes
for Every Occasion

ROBYN CHUBEY

CONTENTS

SPRING

SUMMER

FALL

WINTER

DEAR READER

When I was a child, our little family of four (Mom, Dad, brother, and me) ate together nearly every evening, and my very first chore was setting the table for dinner with my mother's guidance. I remember truly enjoying this responsibility, even as a young girl. My parents were both great cooks, and we always had a variety of meal nights—Italian, Chinese, Mexican, homemade pizza night, casseroles, soups, and all the best staples from my dad's youth, like fried chicken and biscuits, pierogies with fried bacon, and sauerkraut. My dad grew up on a farm with a Georgia-born mom and a Polish-Ukrainian dad, which meant we enjoyed incredible recipes. Food in our home was an event, and adding new recipes was constant.

My parents were also both avid gardeners, and much of what they cooked came from our farm and home gardens. From a young age, I learned that planting, picking, and storing potatoes meant you'd have the best french fries until the spring, and that you could easily grow and keep hundreds of carrots to last fresh until mid-winter. They instilled in me a love for small-scale farming, gardening, food, and gathering at the table with loved ones. But it was my mother's etiquette and style that taught me that a table was always better to gather around when it was beautifully set, and here I am, decades later, still truly loving to do just that.

If you love hosting and planning pretty scenes to enjoy with your family, let this book act as inspiration to meet you where you are and grow with you. I hope it inspires you to create your own wonderful memories around the dinner table. Throughout these pages, there are ideas for decor, crafts, and delicious recipes for every type of holiday, along with non-holiday seasonal celebration ideas to make traditions new and old even more memorable with your loved ones. My hope is that you enjoy following this book from start to finish, get creative, and stay connected to the seasons, all while keeping sustainability in mind.

Each section has a theme, color palette, and flavor profile that is inspired by nature and what's in season, so it is easy to reuse ingredients in multiple ways for each event, making planning simpler and, hopefully, also reducing costs and food waste. There are also tips for ways to prepare ahead, to make preparing for every gathering easier.

You'll also find fun handmade crafts sprinkled throughout each season that you can include in any event or make as gifts for guests. The crafts are meant to be a playful addition to bring an extra layer of charm and creativity to your home and gatherings, but there are no hard and fast rules—just opportunities to experiment and enjoy the process.

You can always mix and match the crafts, swapping them out to suit your mood, your event, or even the supplies you have on hand. Think of them as delightful, interchangeable accents to personalize your seasonal style. Above all, embrace crafting as a chance to have fun, try something new, and create special touches that bring joy to your home and gatherings.

My goal is to share with you my deep love for living seasonally, and how I use all the opportunities and bounties the seasons have to offer to make magical moments to share with friends and family. I hope to inspire you to create new traditions and add to existing ones, all while having lots of fun.

Robyn Chubey

BUILDING A TABLESCAPE COLLECTION

Finding inspiration for beautiful tablescapes is endless—from magazines and books to events, hosting blogs, and social media. I use these sources to gather ideas and recognize themes that resonate with my style. If you are starting from scratch, consider creating a photo file on your phone filled with table and centerpiece images you love—it's a great way to identify your personal style. I often screenshot items I like and use Google's reverse image search to shop smarter. I keep wish lists for both new and secondhand hunts.

To save time and money, and to stay hosting-ready, I recommend starting with a base collection of neutral tablecloths, place settings, and décor. These timeless basics can be reused for various occasions and be dressed up with seasonal accents or personalized touches to suit your aesthetic.

I love having solid classic basics for plates and cutlery while adding unique, thrifted, and secondhand pieces for endless styling options. Sustainability is key—I believe you can create an elegant table while being environmentally conscious. My go-to dish sets include:

* **White hobnob** (10 pieces): dinner plates, side plates, bowls
* **Classic ceramic gray** (8 pieces): dinner plates, side plates, salad bowls, pasta bowls
* **Cream scalloped-edge** (8 pieces): dinner plates, side plates, salad/soup bowls, little side dishes, pasta bowls

I mix and match, especially for bigger gatherings. Thrifted finds add personality and can be re-donated—creative, stylish, and waste-free.

With this in mind, let's dive into table essentials and the items that bring your tablescape vision to life.

TABLE ESSENTIALS

A beautiful tablescape starts with thoughtful layers and a few key pieces. In this section, you'll find the foundational elements—from linens to cutlery—that create a welcoming, stylish table. First up: a list of essential table items every host should have on hand to build a versatile, swoon-worthy setup your guests will love.

* **Tablecloth or table runner:** A tablecloth and/or a table runner is typically the first thing added to a tablescape. It's important to pick your decor colors before starting, as the tablecloth will be crucial to tying the overall look.
* **Centerpiece:** The centerpiece is the star of the show and rests in the middle of the table. A great centerpiece can include a variety of items, from flowers in vessels and vases, to potted plants, seasonal decorative items, and more.
* **Ambiance lighting:** Candles and candleholders, battery lamps, and twinkle lights should be thoughtfully arranged around the table and evenly spaced out for all those seated to enjoy. Always be mindful of safety with lit candles, opting for battery-operated versions when required.
* **Place mats:** Not only do place mats protect your table from spills, but they also enhance its esthetic appeal. They provide an opportunity to layer different elements, adding a touch of formality to your setup. Plus, they're versatile—you can easily swap them out to reflect various holidays, making them a fun and functional addition to your table decor.
* **Dinnerware:** I like to layer a variety of plates and bowls, depending on what I am serving. Typically, smaller bowls and plates go on top of larger plates, and small plates for breads are typically placed to the left, although I often opt to put them where I feel they look and fit best on the table. When you are at home, you can make and break the rules!
* **Cutlery:** The general rule for placing cutlery is forks go to the left of the plate and spoons and knives to the right, but you can get creative with inserting all the cutlery into napkin pockets too.
* **Napkins and napkin rings:** Napkins are either folded or inserted into napkin rings and placed to the left of the forks or on top of the plates.
* **Glassware:** Cups or glasses are placed to the right of the plate, above the knives. Wine glasses are usually placed above the water glasses.
* **Place cards or name tags:** These are optional and can be added as a special or elevated touch.

Getting Creative

My favorite tablescape rule that I like to live by is that almost anything fabric can become a table linen! For tablecloths, any large fabric will do. Simply lay them on the table as they are and voila! They are now tablecloths.

Ideas for things you can use (and that I have used!) include:

* Scarves
* Sheets
* Blankets
* Discount fabric pieces that can be hemmed around the edges (iron-on hem tape works great for non-sewers). I've thrifted a few tablecloths in my collection, I've been passed down a couple, and of course, I've also purchased a few classic linen basics.

Here are some of my favorite ideas for napkin collections:

* Tea towels that you can square off and hem for the cutest print napkins
* Linen fabric cut and sewn into squares
* Linen fabric torn into squares and left with a pretty, frayed edge
* Store-bought napkins from places like H&M Home, HomeGoods, or Homesense

One of my favorite hacks is to add a high-quality coordinating paper napkin to each place setting, tucked into or folded under my cloth napkins, so guests can use their fabric napkin on their lap and their paper napkin more liberally for sticky fingers. This little touch is always appreciated during meals with finger foods.

To elevate your napkin presentation, consider folding your napkins in creative ways for added sophistication. While any napkin can be folded, larger ones, around 18 to 20 inches (46 to 51 centimeters), are much easier to work with than smaller ones. Using an iron to press down the folds can also help them hold their shape better and give your table a polished, elegant finish.

Pocket Napkin Fold

Perfect for any tablescape, this napkin fold is so simple and yet looks elegant. It's best done on lightweight linen napkins that can be pressed, as shown in the photo at the top of page 8.

1. Lay out a square napkin oriented as a diamond with a point at the top and bottom.
2. Fold the left, bottom, and right corners into the center, creating a house shape.
3. Next, take the entire long bottom edge and fold it up to meet the top of the widest space, just under the "triangle roof" of the house shape.
4. Flip the napkin fold over, keeping the point at the top.
5. Fold the top point of the "roof triangle" all the way down to the center of the bottom edge.
6. Fold the bottom point of that triangle once more, bringing it up to meet the new top edge. (It will look like a small triangle in the top center of the large rectangle, touching the top edge.)
7. Flip the napkin over again, this time flipping from the top corners so it's upside down. It will look like a flat, wide rectangle.
8. Fold both side edges to meet in the center, and then fold the side edges into the center a second time. They will feel thick—that's okay—and the shape will now be a tall rectangle.
9. Flip the napkin over from the left, and you will have your perfect napkin pocket to tuck sprigs of herbs or florals into.
10. Press the napkins with an iron, so they stay nice and flat.

Cutlery

When it comes to cutlery, if you are only going to have one set, a high-quality original-finish stainless-steel set is my top recommendation. A matte or hammered handle variety will be extra-durable and withstand dishwashing and frequent long-term use without showing scratches, but polished is beautiful and durable too. You will want to look for 18/10- or 18/8-grade stainless-steel; this grade of stainless is strong, food-safe, corrosion-resistant, and heat-resistant.

Colored stainless-steel cutlery, such as black or gold, is both beautiful and strong when made from 18/10- or 18/8-grade stainless steel. However, these finishes are less durable and more prone to wear over time. If you choose these options, you may need to handle them with extra care or replace them more frequently.

For my own collection, I use a high-quality stainless-steel set with a hammered handle style, which is both durable and photogenic. I love that it doesn't show scratches or reflections, making it practical and low-maintenance. For special occasions, I bring out my matte copper or gold cutlery sets. I care for these pieces carefully by handwashing and using them sparingly, which has kept them looking beautiful for many years.

Bow Napkin Fold

Here are my tips for creating a cute and simple bow fold for your tablescape.

1. From the backside of the napkin, fold one end up a third of the way, then fold the other end over it to create a long rectangle.
2. With the seam toward you, use a metal tie, twist-tie, or any twine to cinch the middle point together, creating the bow center.
3. With the seam and tie knot facing you, fold the two corners on the left side into the center line to meet one another, forming a point. Fold the point toward the center of the napkin and tuck it in, creating one side of the bow.
4. Repeat the process on the right side to create the other side of the bow.
5. Flip the napkin over and add any decor to the center, such as a berry cluster, if desired.

Place Mats

Place mats are fun, and they can be used with or without tablecloths. My favorite natural place mats include:

* **Wood:** Rustic and timeless, wood is great for cozy dinners or nature-inspired tablescapes.
* **Wicker**: Light and airy, wicker is ideal for a coastal or boho vibe and works well for casual brunches and outdoor gatherings.
* **Seagrass:** Organic and textured, seagrass brings a relaxed, earthy feel.
* **Jute:** Neutral and versatile, jute adds a natural warmth and pairs well with minimalist, rustic, or casual everyday dining.
* **Rattan:** Chic and woven, rattan offers a refined yet natural touch.

The earthy tones of these place mats pair so well with other wood and wicker table decor and add a neutral break when you're decorating with a lot of color. I love that you can layer these over any color or pattern and they'll still look fabulous; they are like the blue jeans of table fashion.

Round, single-color, simple place mats are also great options. The round style allows more space between place settings and is a great shape to complement the plates and create a repeat of patterns. They are also available for a very reasonable price at most dollar stores and online, meaning you can grab a few key colors (such as green, yellow, and black). They are also super thin, making it easy to store them.

Centerpieces

Before purchasing any new items, I love to "shop my home," exploring spaces like the bedrooms, living room, and kitchen for centerpieces and table decor. I often shuffle decorative items from room to room and season to season to maximize their use while minimizing storage needs—candleholders in my bedroom from January to March might find their way into the kitchen or onto the table from April to June. When I need additional pieces to complete my creative vision for holiday or table decor, I usually start by visiting local thrift stores or checking Facebook Marketplace for unique or vintage finds. After that, I head to Homesense (Canada's version of HomeGoods) and then browse online at my favorite stores like H&M Home or Zara Home. For particularly specific items, I rely on Google's reverse image search or Amazon's image search to find the perfect piece.

When looking for centerpiece items and table decor to add to your collection, the top things to keep an eye out for are:

* Vases (ceramic in white or earth tones, colored glass, wood, and wicker)
* Candles and candleholders
* Faux floral picks, berry picks, or foliage picks
* Twinkle lights
* Garlands
* Fresh or faux plants and flowers
* Salt and pepper shakers or grinders
* Baskets for bread or other offerings
* Pitchers
* Little bowls or dishes with toppings or condiments
* Cake stands and cloches
* Napkin rings

And of course, you want to use any greenery, herbs, fruits, vegetables, or other natural elements to complete the look. Don't be afraid to think outside of the box and use unique or quirky items on your tablescapes—experimenting is the best way to spark ideas and refine your personal style.

SEASONAL LIVING AND INSPIRATIONS

Now that we've covered the essentials of building and creating tablescape inspiration, let's explore additional design elements and things to consider while decorating your home for each season or event. From mastering the art of seasonal decor with captivating tablescapes to edible flowers, this chapter walks you through my four simple table decor rules, equipment lists, and more. Let's get started!

FOUR RULES FOR CREATIVE DESIGNS

When I set out to create a beautiful tablescape, floral arrangement, room, or vignette, (which is a fancy word for a styled setup of items like you'd see at a coffee station or on a sideboard), there are four simple design rules that I like to follow, which I will detail below. All these rules are set to accomplish one thing—to appease the human eye.

When looking at a layout, your eyes want to easily find a focal point (in the case of a tablescape this will likely be the floral arrangement) and a natural flow. If the flow is disrupted by empty spaces, misplaced items, overcrowding, or overwhelming elements, it's a cue to review your design and make adjustments.

1. Focal Point

Choosing a focal point is key to guiding the eye—on a table, it can be a single large arrangement at the center or a spread-out centerpiece of low arrangements. In bouquets, this is often a standout focal flower with supporting blooms around it.

The focal point is also where you can get creative, even breaking the rules with a bold, unique element. It is the star of the setup, supported by the rest of the scene, so keep that in mind as you design the whole view.

2. Balance

Balance ensures all elements feel evenly distributed and harmonious in a scene. For example, if you're using black accents like a vase, baskets, and salt and pepper shakers, avoid clustering them on one side. Instead, spread them out to guide the eye smoothly across the layout. Similarly, a large red rose arrangement at the table's center might feel overpowering if paired with bold red napkins on the plates. Instead, opt for a subtle red detail, like a napkin ring or berry pick, for a more balanced look.

Symmetry also plays a key role in achieving balance. Avoid placing the main floral arrangement off-center on the table or plates misaligned on place mats. If you have a tall candle holder on one side, balance it with a similar (not necessarily identical) one on the opposite side to maintain harmony.

3. Negative Space

Negative space simply refers to the empty areas around and between objects in a design or layout. It's crucial to have adequate spaces between items, whether it's tabletop or counter space, wall space in a room, or air in a floral arrangement.

I often compare this to being in a thrift store where items are piled high—even if they're organized into sections, it's hard to focus on any one thing clearly. This sense of clutter can leave people feeling lost and frustrated, which is why many struggle to find what they're looking for and walk away feeling overwhelmed. It's often a case of less is more!

4. Repeating Elements

As I start gathering core items for my design, my main objective is to tie these main elements with other items within the scene, creating a unified and cohesive feel. Characteristics for these main elements fall under a few basic categories:

* Color
* Pattern
* Texture
* Shape

In practical use, if I'm starting with an arrangement for the center of a tablescape, and I choose a white vase and a red floral, I now have the job of linking that central piece to the rest of the table by adding additional white and red elements. If I choose to have round place mats, I'll want to add round plates and round glasses to my layout, and if I have chosen wicker for my chargers, I'll pop in wicker baskets around the scene.

Ideally, you will have three items linked to one another, or three repeating elements, happening around the scene for each additional element you add. This means in a floral arrangement, if you add one yellow flower then you then need two or more yellow flowers to balance it. In my experience there is no limit to how many elements you can have repeating, but that brings me to my next rule!

Be Creative and Have Fun

Play is so important to creativity. Trying new things is what leads to breakthroughs in personal style and amazing new creations. There's nothing wrong with having some design fails, as long as you are having fun. Give yourself permission to experiment on your design journey. Why not take some risks?!

PLANNING YOUR TABLE DECOR

Now that we've covered all the essential items and design guidance for your table, let's dive into the planning process. When organizing my table decor, I follow a simple yet effective recipe to ensure seamless results every time.

To kickstart the creative process, I begin by selecting one defining piece of decor that will inspire the rest of the setup. This might be a stunning new tablecloth with a unique print, fresh florals just hitting their prime in my garden, a vibrant vase, or playful citrus picks perfect for accentuating a napkin fold. Typically, I start with flowers—they often serve as the centerpiece for most decor sections in this book. This defining element becomes the foundation for the entire design and makes the process far more intuitive.

Once I've chosen my focal piece, I move on to gathering complementary items. Linens, flatware, candles, and other accents are brought together to form a cohesive "living mood board." This allows me to see how all the elements work together and identify any additional items I might need. With all the essentials in hand, I can then begin the setup.

Steps for Setting Up

Here's a quick guide for how to set up your table.

1. **Tablecloth and base layers:** Start by laying out the tablecloth and runner, along with any base elements like garlands or greenery. Leave enough space on each side for place mats and place settings. If the centerpiece extends too far into the place settings, consider skipping the place mats or layering them carefully under the centerpiece.
2. **Centerpiece assembly:** Arrange vases and florals, nestling them into garlands or centering them on the runner. Add candles and any seasonal decorative touches, along with practical elements such as salt and pepper shakers.
3. **Place settings:** Finally, set out the plates, cutlery, glassware, and napkins to complete the look. While etiquette suggests keeping the table free of unused items during meals, there's no harm in adding creative touches like decorative bowls or extra plates. It's your design—let it reflect your style and vision!

Once your table is ready, take a moment to review the overall design, ensuring it aligns with the cohesive principles discussed earlier in this book (pages 12 to 13). Make any necessary adjustments and admire your work.

MUST-GROW EDIBLE FLOWERS

Cooking and crafting with flowers are among my favorite creative activities. In this section, I share my favorite edible flowers that are easy to grow, low-cost, and low-maintenance. These flowers will keep producing all season and, if you let them go to seed, you can collect and replant them for free year after year. To enjoy them in winter, simply press and dry the flowers, then store them in a dark, dry place for later use. Here are ten easy edible flowers to grow and my favorite ways to use them.

1. **Feverfew:** This herb is known for its medicinal properties and has a bitter taste. Safe when consumed only in small quantities, it is a beautiful garnish on salads, charcuterie boards, cakes, and cookies (although I would personally pull it off before eating due to its bitter taste).
2. **Bee balm:** Also known as bergamot or wild bergamot, bee balm is a fragrant herb with a citrusy, minty, and slightly spicy flavor. The fresh or dried leaves can be used as a substitute for oregano or thyme in recipes like soups, stews, and marinades, and it adds depth to grilled meats, vegetables, and salads. It can also be used as a cut flower.
3. **Zinnias:** These popular edible garden flowers are known for their vibrant colors, but they also offer a subtle flavor and bright decorative uses in recipes, which makes them a great addition to mixed greens or fruit salads. Their petals can be sprinkled over salads and side dishes for a pop of color. Zinnias can also serve as elegant garnishes for platters, drinks, or desserts. And they are excellent cut flowers that can last up to three weeks in a vase.
4. **Marigolds:** These vibrant flowers, with a mildly citrusy, tangy, and slightly bitter taste, have a wide range of edible uses. The petals can be added to fresh salads for a burst of color and a hint of citrusy tang, and they work as a garnish on savory dishes, desserts, and cocktails. Marigold petals can also be mixed into rice or grain dishes for visual appeal and a subtle flavor, and can even be used as a natural food dye for a saffron-like yellow hue. The petals are lovely incorporated into breads, muffins, or cookies, and they also make a gorgeous addition to arrangements and centerpieces.
5. **Nasturtiums:** These flowers are widely used in cooking due to their peppery and slightly spicy flavor. You can eat the leaves, stems, and flowers, and even their seeds, pickled, as capers! The vibrant blossoms are used to decorate soups, desserts, and cocktail glasses, and they can also be stuffed with cheese as an appetizer; later in these pages, you will find a great recipe for Nasturtium Vinaigrette (page 120). They are also a favorite of mine to grow for their voluminous, cascading radiance in pots and in the garden, producing blooms all summer long.
6. **Calendula:** This flower is loved for its mild, earthy flavor and vibrant yellow-to-orange petals. Its versatility makes it a popular edible flower. You can use the petals sprinkled over salads for a splash of color and a slightly tangy taste, or finely chop them and mix into butter or cream cheese for a colorful spread. You can use these pretty blossoms to decorate cakes, cookies, or, as I do later in this book, donuts (page 147).

NOTE

Keep in mind to always use organic, pesticide-free flowers and be aware of any potential allergies to new foods.

7. **Runner beans:** Runner beans are excellent to use as a garnish on dishes, desserts, and salads. They have a delicate, mildly sweet flavor with a faint, grassy undertone. The sweetness is subtle, not overpowering, and they also carry a slight hint of the fresh bean taste, which the flowers will turn into if left on the vine!
8. **Pansies and violas:** These are versatile edible flowers that can add a touch of elegance and flavor to a variety of dishes. In salads, they add a splash of color and a delicate flavor. You can use them to beautifully decorate cakes, cupcakes, ice cream, and candied pansies. They can also be used as a sweet and colorful topping for desserts. They are gorgeous pressed and dried to use in crafts and cooking in the winter months, and they are beautiful in arrangements.
9. **Gomphrena:** Also known as globe amaranth, gomphrena is an edible flower with a variety of culinary uses. It has a mild, slightly sweet flavor that carries a floral note. This vibrant, papery flower adds a pop of color to salads, desserts, and cocktails. If you grow purple ones, the blossoms can be used to create natural food coloring. Gomphrena is an incredible dried flower, keeping its shape and color easily. It's drought-tolerant and adds texture to arrangements.
10. **Chamomile:** One of my favorites for its country charm, chamomile has a mild, sweet, and slightly apple-like flavor. It's often described as having a calming and soothing effect and is best known for its use in herbal teas. Chamomile flowers can be used to flavor a variety of dishes, including soups, stews, and desserts, and they can also be added to baked goods like cakes and cookies. But I love them most as an adorable garnish and in a vase, spilling out as a giant wild bouquet.

The ideal time to sow most of the flowers on this list is early spring after the last frost, when the ground is cool and workable. Flowers like feverfew, bee balm, marigolds, nasturtiums, calendula, gomphrena, and chamomile should be planted during this time. Pansies and violas thrive in early spring when the soil is cool and there's still a chance of light frost, or even in early fall in warmer regions for spring blooms. For flowers such as zinnias and runner beans, sow them in spring when the soil is warm with temperatures around 70°F to 80°F (21°C to 27°C).

ESSENTIAL TOOLS & EQUIPMENT LISTS

In the pages to follow you will find so many great recipes and crafts. This is everything you will need to create them.

For Crafts:

* Permanent markers or paint pens, in black or metallic colors
* Scissors
* Elastics
* Jute twine
* Burlap or other decorative fabrics for jar lids
* Jam jars or other giftable jars
* Small and medium lidded containers
* Hot-glue gun
* Small wooden beads
* Bottle ice mold
* Pint jars with lids
* Card stock
* Waxed paper
* Letter stamps
* Metal poker or skewer
* Secateurs (pruning shears)
* Utility knife
* Cricut cutting machine
* Sticker paper

For Recipes:

* A variety of glass syrup or oil jars with stoppers
* Measuring cups and spoons
* A variety of serving boards and charcuterie boards
* A variety of serving bowls, small to large
* Piping bag and small to large star and round tips
* Melon baller
* Skewers
* Mixing bowls from small to large
* 12-cup muffin pan
* Bar set, with muddler and cocktail shaker
* 9-inch (23 cm) pie pan
* 13 × 18-inch (33 × 46 cm) baking sheet
* 9 × 13-inch (23 × 33 cm) baking pan
* Loaf pans
* Bundt cake pan
* Donut baking pan
* Whisk
* Round cookie cutters, 2-inch (5 cm), 2.5-inch (6 cm), 3-inch (7.5 cm), and 4-inch (10 cm)
* Heart-shaped cookie cutters, 2-inch (5 cm), 3-inch (8 cm), and 4-inch (10 cm)
* Stand mixer or electric hand mixer
* Knife set
* Rolling pin
* Cast-iron skillet, medium
* Stainless-steel pan, large
* Dutch oven
* Frying pans, small, medium, and large
* Baking dish, 8 × 10-inch (20 × 25 cm) or 9 × 9-inch (23 × 23 cm)
* Food processor
* Vegetable peeler
* Blender
* Pots, small, medium, and large
* Teapot and kettle
* Tea towels
* Dough cutter
* Pizza cutter
* Plastic wrap
* Cookie bags
* Box grater
* Loaf pan

SPRING

At the first signals of warmer days, my hosting- and harvesting-loving heart refills with the inspiration that had dwindled through the final weeks of winter. Rhubarb, spring onion, lilac, and asparagus are just some of the key flavors that emerge in early spring and scream “A new season is here!” These scents and tastes snap me into an invigorated energy, and that’s why I love to include them in my first gatherings of the year. Creating and sharing traditions that include all my best memories that this season has to offer is one of my favorite ways to celebrate.

EASTER BRUNCH

When I was a child, only two holidays carried with them the excitement of family gatherings and the childhood wonder of mythical visitors bringing gifts—Christmas and Easter. Easter, being the first of the year, was a wonderful main event to ring in the spring. There was something magical about kicking off a cool (and possibly frigid!) spring day with a bunny leaving chocolate eggs all around the house for me to find, followed by me dressing up in my Sunday best and heading for a delicious brunch with family.

These days, it's the excitement of hosting this egg-tastic celebration that gives me the same sense of joy that I felt when I was little.

In the following pages, I hope you find new inspirations, from the beautiful decor ideas to some of my favorite delicious recipes to incorporate into your own celebrations as you continue adding to your family's traditions.

AN EGG-CEPTIONAL CELEBRATION

Creating an Easter tablescape is a delightful way to combine your creativity and traditions while bringing the beauty of spring into your home. Planning your Easter table setup before decorating helps you choose a theme and color scheme that can inspire and guide the rest of your home decor, ensuring a cohesive and harmonious look. Here are my tips for creating an egg-ceptional table.

Florals

Since Easter often falls in early spring, sometimes as soon as the first week, I usually begin by selecting florals for the table and building my palette from there. The availability of fresh flowers varies in early spring, so it's best to follow Mother Nature's lead. Visiting your grocer, garden center, or florist shortly before your event lets you adapt your plans based on what's available. Some of my top Easter floral recommendations are:

* **Tulips:** A quintessential Easter flower, symbolizing happiness, love, rebirth, and good luck. Their egg-shaped blooms evoke Easter eggs. These are best in white or yellow.
* **Daffodils:** Early spring bloomers that symbolize good luck, love, respect, and the renewal of life after winter.
* **Lilies:** These represent purity, rebirth, and hope, often linked to Christ's resurrection and Easter traditions.
* **Pansies:** Frost-tolerant and vibrant, these flowers symbolize love and remembrance, making them a perfect Easter choice.
* **High-quality faux flowers:** They allow for flexibility and advance preparation, ensuring long-lasting, stunning displays.

TIPS ON USING FAUX FLOWERS

If you are using artificial flowers, here are my tips to help you make them look more natural and give them an elegant feel.

* Search for "real touch" artificial flowers. These faux flowers are made with realistic-looking and real-feeling leaves and petals that are not only flexible, but they're also long-lasting and great for storage. I prefer these to silk or fabric flowers, even if that means sticking to certain flower types, such as tulips.
* Bend the artificial stems to have the blooms fall or cascade in different directions. This helps make your arrangements look their very best, as real flowers would. Cut the stems or bend them to different heights in your arrangements.
* Mix faux florals in with real ones, along with real or faux greenery. Don't be afraid to pop a couple of potted hyacinths or fresh daffodils into the scene to create a "new-to-you" beautiful floral setting each year.

Using high-quality faux florals is such an easy way to have a beautiful display, while also being economical and sustainable.

Colors

When designing your Easter tablescape, incorporate bright greens, oranges, or white paired with grassy and earthy tones. For florals, these colors work great to create a fresh and inviting springtime look:

* **White:** Versatile and timeless, ideal for tulips, daffodils, and lilies.
* **Yellows and oranges:** Vibrant shades that add a cheerful touch. Daffodils, tulips, and pansies are great choices in these colors.
* **Pastels:** Soft hues like pinks, blues, and purples for classic elegance. Tulips and pansies are the best in these colors.
* **Greens:** Great for natural accents, such as moss runners.

Centerpieces and Decor Suggestions

Your centerpiece is the heart of your tablescape and should harmonize with your chosen colors and theme. Whether simple or elaborate, it sets the tone for the overall look. Complement bright spring colors or crisp whites with vessels and decor in neutral or earthy tones, such as:

* Soft moss green
* Warm terra-cotta
* Neutral tan
* Muted browns
* Whites and creams

Use these tones in your centerpieces and decor through:

* Terra-cotta pots, planters, tureens, or vases
* Trays, cake stands, and wooden boards
* Candles: pillar or taper candles in whites, brights, or pastels for added warmth and glow
* Holiday-themed decor, such as rabbit figurines or eggs (real or faux) in earthy materials or coordinating colors for a charming touch

Most of these supplies can easily be found at craft stores like Michaels or Hobby Lobby. These arrangements and decor ideas are sure to bring elegance and harmony to your Easter-inspired dining table.

Tablecloth

Tablecloths add sophistication, softness, and warmth, providing the canvas for your creative vision. Here are my suggested tablecloth selections for Easter:

* **Neutral or pastel linen tablecloths:** Choosing a soft white, pale gray, or cream tablecloth in a natural linen will add a certain softness to your table design, but this choice will also allow the rest of your decor to stand out. Perfect for when you want something simple yet classic.
* **Patterned tablecloths:** A patterned option is great for adding some Easter charm to your space. When using bold patterns on your tablecloth, like geometric patterns or bunny or egg motifs, you can either keep the decor and florals subtle and elegant or go big and pair with lots of coordinating Easter-themed items.

Place Settings

Place mats and cutlery are important for enhancing the elegance of an Easter theme. For place mats and napkins, let your tablecloth inspire you, and either coordinate to the patterns in a solid option or use a neutral-toned or natural place mat like jute or bamboo to tie in other earthy items in your design. I recommend the following cutlery pieces for a layer of sophistication:

* **Silver:** This is great if you have chosen cool, crisp tones on your table like whites or pastel blues. It also looks great with bright oranges or greens.
* **Gold:** This is the ideal option if you have opted for pinks or lavenders on your table. Gold also pairs well with warm neutrals.
* **Copper:** This selection looks great with earthy tones, warm neutrals, or a palette of pastel greens.

Lila
Dad
Cade
Mom

EGG PLACE MARKERS

If you are looking for a simple way to have your guests feel welcome and special at your table, add place markers! Whenever I use them, I'm always met with little exclamations of appreciation from kids and adults alike. It's so wonderful as a guest not to have to ask where you are sitting; it solves confusion and looks so thoughtful. For Easter, these egg table markers are simple yet elegant!

Faux eggs or hard-boiled eggs
Permanent marker, acrylic paint, or paint pen (colors of your choice)
Egg holders (optional)
1 or 2 small bowls per guest
Moss

1. Write your guests' names on the eggs using either a permanent marker, acrylic paint, or a paint pen.
2. Add small designs or patterns to the eggs or have your kids get creative with markers or paints to add names and designs especially made for each guest.
3. Place each egg holder into a small bowl, then set the designed eggs in the egg holders and surround the base of the holders with moss. If you do not have egg holders, place the eggs into small bowls, surrounding their bases with moss.
4. Place the place markers on your table setting.

TIPS

You can find egg holders in season either online, at thrift stores, or at dollar stores. If you have a Cricut machine, you can use it to add the names of your guests on the eggs. If you are using faux eggs, they can be given as gifts to your guests, especially if they were decorated by the kids, or, as I prefer to do, store them along with all of your Easter decor for use each year.

RHUBARB COFFEE-CAKE STREUSEL MUFFINS

TOTAL TIME: 40 MINUTES **YIELD:** 12 MUFFINS

If you have never been a rhubarb fan or if you have never tried it, this is the recipe that will make you fall in love with rhubarb. The tart and tangy rhubarb flavor in these moist muffins is so balanced by the sweet cinnamon streusel that it creates a muffin experience like no other. This recipe is very much like a coffee cake, but with a fresh twist. All spring long, these are on repeat in my home.

FOR THE MUFFINS

1½ cups (180 g) all-purpose flour
½ cup (100 g) granulated sugar
1 teaspoon salt
2 teaspoons baking powder
1 teaspoon ground cinnamon
1 large egg
⅓ cup (80 ml) vegetable oil
⅓ cup (80 ml) 2% milk
1½ cups (188 g) finely diced fresh rhubarb, plus more for toppings

FOR THE STREUSEL TOPPING

½ cup (100 g) granulated sugar
⅓ cup (40 g) all-purpose flour
¼ cup (½ stick, or 55 g) unsalted butter, cold, cubed into ¼-inch (6 mm) pieces
1 teaspoon ground cinnamon

FOR THE ICING (OPTIONAL)

½ cup (60 g) confectioners' sugar
1 tablespoon 2% milk

1. Preheat the oven to 375°F (190°C). Line a 12-cup muffin pan with paper liners.
2. To make the muffins: In a large mixing bowl, whisk together the flour, sugar, salt, baking powder, and cinnamon. In a separate medium mixing bowl, whisk together the egg, oil, and milk. Pour the wet mixture into the dry mixture, stirring to combine. Add the diced rhubarb and fold it into the batter. Using a spoon, drop equal amounts of batter into each paper liner.
3. To make the streusel: In a small bowl, add the sugar, flour, butter, and cinnamon. Using a fork, press the butter into the flour and sugar until mixed; it will look lumpy and coarse.
4. Top the muffin batter with equal amounts of the streusel and a few more pieces of the diced rhubarb.
5. Bake for 20 to 25 minutes, until a toothpick inserted into the center of a muffin comes out clean. Transfer to a wire rack to cool completely, about 15 minutes.
6. To make the icing: In a medium bowl, mix the confectioners' sugar and milk then, using a spoon or piping bag, drizzle zigzag stripes across the muffins and serve.

TIPS

You can replace the Miracle Whip with mayonnaise if preferred. Get creative with the look of your eggs by adding more bacon or dicing your onion into little green “onion sprinkles.” Also, if you don’t want to remove the entire egg white from the yolk, you can instead cut the eggs in half through the whole thing.

MUSTARD CAVIAR EGG BITES

TOTAL TIME: 30 MINUTES **YIELD:** 12 DEVILED EGG HALVES

This esthetic spin on traditional deviled eggs is one that will have everyone oohing, ahhing, and mmmmming. They are tangy and textured and elevate the typical deviled egg to something special, while being much simpler to make than they look. If you have ever made traditional deviled eggs, you'll find that piping the fluffy yolk mixture back in with a pastry bag makes it not only look more elegant, but it's also much faster!

- 1 teaspoon salt
- 6 large eggs
- 1 tablespoon yellow mustard, plus more for taste
- 1 tablespoon Miracle Whip, plus more for consistency
- 1 tablespoon white vinegar, plus more for taste
- 4 to 5 teaspoons Mustard Caviar (see page 205)
- 1 large green onion, cut into 1½-inch (4 cm) pieces
- 4 slices bacon, cooked and diced into crumble-size pieces (¼ to ½ inch, or 6 to 13 mm)

1. To make the eggs: Fill a medium pot with water and the salt and eggs. Bring to a boil over high heat, then reduce the heat to medium-high and cook for 10 minutes. Remove the pot from the heat and drain. Run cold water over the eggs for 2 to 3 minutes. Knock each egg on a hard surface a few times to crack the shells, then peel them.
2. Using a knife, slice a ⅛-inch (3 mm) sliver off the top and bottom of each egg to create flat edges. Cut the eggs in half widthwise by sliding the knife around the circumference of the eggs to remove the egg whites. This ensures the egg whites easily pull off the yolk.
3. Place all the egg whites on their flat bottoms in a medium serving dish, and place all the egg yolks in a separate medium bowl.
4. Add the mustard, Miracle Whip, and vinegar to the egg yolks. Mix well until the yolks have a stiff but smooth consistency. If the consistency seems dry, add another teaspoon of mustard or Miracle Whip, alternating with one or the other until it feels smooth enough to pipe nicely.
5. Fill a piping bag fitted with a tip of your choice with the egg mixture. Pipe the egg mixture into each hollowed egg white, swirling upward, leaving a little gap on one side, then spoon the mustard caviar into the gap.
6. Top with a piece of green onion and a bit of crumbled bacon. Enjoy!

RECIPE

PROSCIUTTO, MINT & MELON SKEWERS

TOTAL TIME: 20 MINUTES **YIELD:** 16 SKEWERS

Nothing brings the fun to an appetizer like a melon baller. As a kitchen tool, its history and origins are unclear. Legend has it that in nineteenth-century France, chefs graced us with the invention, and from that moment on, party appetizers were forever elevated. I imagine the first ballroom parties featuring melon balls, with exclamations of *"Trop mignon!"* echoing through the kitchens and halls. I have to say, with the flavor and color combination in the recipe to follow, I have a feeling your tablemates will be exclaiming, "Too cute!" once again.

1 ripe large cantaloupe
1 ripe large honeydew
8 slices prosciutto
16 bocconcini cheese balls
32 mint leaves

1. To make the melon balls: Slice the cantaloupe and honeydew melons in half and remove the seeds. Using a high-quality, sturdy metal melon baller, work from the inside of the melons. Sink the melon baller at an angle into the flesh. Once, it's pressed in as far as it can go, twist and scoop to create the balls. Don't worry if your melon ball isn't perfectly round; they typically aren't ever perfect on all sides. Simply place the imperfect side down in a bowl, and no one will ever notice.
2. To make the prosciutto rosettes: Cut the prosciutto slices in half lengthwise, then fold the long strips again lengthwise, to create a smooth top edge on one side. Starting at either end of the prosciutto strip, gently roll it up to form a rosette.
3. To make the skewers: Slide the melon balls (imperfect side down) onto the skewers and alternate with prosciutto and cheese.
4. Place a fresh mint leaf on either side of each prosciutto rosette and enjoy.

TIPS

To save prep time, melon balls can be made up to 3 days in advance, then covered and refrigerated. You can make this recipe a day before and cover, but I recommend waiting to add the fresh mint leaves until a few hours before serving.

RECIPE

HAM & CHEESE SCONES

TOTAL TIME: 35 MINUTES **YIELD:** 8 SCONES

An easy recipe that comes together quickly and results in perfection is worth memorizing and making again and again. And that's exactly what you get with these flaky, buttery scones. They are a hearty and satiating savory offering for a brunch spread, and they look so impressive. I love that you can pretend that you spent a lot of time on them, when it's our secret just how easy they are.

- 2 cups (240 g) all-purpose flour, plus more for dusting
- 1 tablespoon granulated sugar
- 1 tablespoon baking powder
- ½ teaspoon black pepper
- ½ teaspoon salt
- ½ cup (1 stick, or 115 g) cold unsalted butter, cut into ¼-inch (6 mm) cubes
- ¾ cup (180 ml) buttermilk
- 1 cup (115 g) shredded cheddar cheese
- ¾ cup (115 g) diced ham
- ¼ cup (11 g) chopped fresh chives

1. Preheat the oven to 425°F (220°C). Line a baking sheet with parchment paper.
2. In a large bowl, whisk together the flour, sugar, baking powder, pepper, and salt. Add the butter cubes to the bowl and, using your fingers, work the butter into the dry ingredients until it becomes a crumbly mixture.
3. Stir in the buttermilk, cheese, ham, and chives until a soft dough forms.
4. Lightly flour a clean work surface, then drop the dough onto it. Knead the dough gently a few times until it comes together; it should have a soft but slightly sticky consistency that holds together well but is a bit moist. If the dough feels too wet, lightly flour your hands or the work surface, gently kneading until combined. Avoid overworking to ensure the scones remain flaky.
5. Using your hands or a rolling pin, roll out the dough into an 8-inch (20 cm) circle about 1 ½ inches (4 cm) thick. Cut the dough circle into 8 wedges and place them onto the prepared baking sheet.
6. Bake for 18 to 20 minutes, until the scones are lightly browned, fluffy, and firm. Serve warm.

TIP

Feel free to substitute the ham with cooked and diced bacon or thickly sliced and diced smoked deli chicken.

RECIPE

RHUBARB MOJITO

TOTAL TIME: 20 MINUTES **YIELD:** 1 MOJITO PLUS 1 CUP (240 ML) OF SIMPLE SYRUP

This cocktail is the perfect complement to the flavors in the preceding Easter recipes, and it's also a drink that's meant to be enjoyed all spring! This refreshing Rhubarb Mojito combines the tartness of rhubarb with a burst of minty freshness, making it the perfect sip to kick off any gathering. It's a drink that brings together the vibrant flavors of the season in every glass.

FOR THE RHUBARB SIMPLE SYRUP

¾ cup (180 ml) cold water
½ cup (100 g) granulated sugar
1 cup (122 g) diced rhubarb

FOR THE MOJITO

10 mint leaves, plus more for garnish (optional)
¼ cup (60 ml) fresh lime juice
1 medium lime, sliced into ¼-inch (6mm) slices, divided
6 tablespoons (90 ml) Rhubarb Simple Syrup
2 tablespoons white rum or gin
Ice cubes or crushed ice
½ cup (120 ml) sparkling water or club soda

1. To make the Rhubarb Simple Syrup: In a small saucepan, stir together the water, sugar, and rhubarb. Bring to a boil over medium-high heat, then reduce the heat to a high simmer, and cook, stirring frequently, for 5 to 10 minutes, until the rhubarb starts to melt into the liquid. Blend well, then strain through a mesh sieve. Pour the liquid into a jar and seal.
2. To make the mojito: Drop the mint leaves into a tall cocktail glass and cover with the lime juice.
3. Using a muddler or the top end of a wooden spoon, muddle, press, or squish the mint into the lime juice in the bottom of a glass to release the mint oil into the juice.
4. Add a couple slices of lime, the rhubarb syrup, and the rum or gin, then add ice cubes or crushed ice.
5. Top with sparkling water or club soda. Garnish with lots of lime slices and mint.
6. Give it a swirl and enjoy!

NOTE

The rhubarb simple syrup can stay in the fridge for 2 to 3 weeks.

MOTHER'S DAY BRUNCH

Mother's Day is one of my favorite gatherings to style, as it encourages femininity. But I must say, if you are a mother hosting a brunch for the moms in your life, it can be a bit of a tricky event. After all, it's supposed to be a day to celebrate ourselves, and it can be tough to feel celebrated when you are cooking, prepping, and setting up a table for guests.

For Mother's Day hosting, I like to use every opportunity to prepare as much as I can in advance to make the morning of the event simple and quick. From setting up the table the evening before (or a few days beforehand if you have another space to eat), to prepping all the vegetables, to premaking pie dough, baking, and freezing dessert ingredients in advance. Doing this ensures you have a relaxed morning of minimal cooking before the doorbell rings.

MOM'S DAY SOIREE

Mother's Day is the perfect occasion to celebrate grace and elegance with large bouquets and charming, dainty table settings. I love adding flowers with fragrance and creating an elegant, layered presentation. Being surrounded by all the lovely details makes this gathering as enjoyable for me as it is to share with my own mom and mother-in-law.

As you gather around your own beautifully arranged table, let the thoughtful details and loving ambiance create a memorable experience. From elegant dishware to lush centerpieces, each element should be designed to celebrate the special bond we share with our mothers, with a healthy dose of feminine style. The following are my tips for creating a table that envelopes the soft hues and elegance of this special season for the special moms in our lives.

Colors and Florals

Purple is one of the earliest spring colors to appear in nature across North America, with blooms like crocuses, violets, and lilacs showcasing stunning violet hues. Along with classic whites, yellows, and greens, purple adds a rich, natural touch to a Mother's Day tablescape.

As I love to honor nature and consider what feels connected to nature when choosing my decor for table settings (and for the rest of my home in each season), I recommend the following violet-hued florals for your Mother's Day brunch tablescape:

* **Purple crocuses:** These flowers symbolize joy, renewal, and youthfulness, blooming early in spring, as a sign of fresh beginnings.
* **Grape hyacinths (muscari):** These flowers signify trust, gratitude, and deep connection. Their small, clustered blooms create a unique and delicate look in potted arrangements.

Pink is another color that works beautifully for a feminine theme. I recommend the following florals, which come in both pink and purple colors:

* **Light purple or pink hyacinths:** These flowers represent peace, beauty, and devotion. Their strong fragrance also adds a lovely touch to any setting.
* **Purple or pink tulips:** These flowers symbolize admiration, perfect for expressing appreciation and deep respect for mothers.
* **Pink or violet-hued Lilacs:** These signify first love and nostalgia, making it a meaningful choice for honoring a mother's love and cherished memories.

Adding pops of white florals, or using the above florals all in white shades for your display, is also a great way to create an elegant and fresh spring mood.

Foraging Lilacs

Lilacs are my personal favorite spring flowers and my favorites to use for Mother's Day celebrations. I love them so much that I named my spring-born daughter Lila, in their honor! The flowers are easy to grow, fragrant, and completely edible, making them the most delicious flavor addition to any spring spread. If you don't have any lilacs in your yard, try asking local businesses or neighbors if you could cut a few branches. Pruning is good for the shrub, and I've had more lilacs than I know what to do with just by asking if I can snip a few where I see them growing prolifically.

There are a few things you need to know when collecting lilacs for arrangements.

* Bring a good strong pair of secateurs or snips. Ideally, you will want to pick them when the blossoms are half open near the base and more closed near the tips, but anytime will do so long as they aren't browning.
* Cut branches with blooms on an angle, allowing 12 inches (30 cm) of woody stem.
* Place them in a basket (a laundry basket works well!). If you're within a 20-minute drive home in a cool vehicle, you won't need to place them in water right away.
* At home, you will want to use your snips to cut a 2-inch (5 cm) split into the base of the stem/branch, which will go into the water in your vase. This long split will help the branches uptake the water they need to stay fresh.
* Fill your vase plentifully with water and remove leaves under the water line.

With this care, your lilacs should stay lovely for several days, and their fragrance will easily fill any space they're in.

Centerpieces and Decor Suggestions

To elevate your Mother's Day tablescape, pair violet-toned florals with elegant vessels that enhance their beauty. Consider the following options:

* Purple-hued ceramic or glass vases for a sophisticated, monochromatic look
* Green or clear glass vases for a simple, natural esthetic
* White ceramic pots topped with moss or rocks for a fresh, clean feel
* Silver or gold vases for a touch of vintage elegance

This thoughtful pairing of vessels and florals ensures a cohesive and visually stunning display.

When creating a centerpiece, a series of vases in varying sizes adds depth and interest to your table. For my setup, I used a large white vase in the center, flanked by two smaller glass vases, all overflowing with foraged lilacs.

To further enhance the ambiance, incorporate taper candles and holders. Green or purple candles work beautifully to echo the springtime palette. For my table, I used sage-green taper candles in silver holders, placed between the vases to coordinate with my white and sage-green tablecloth. I added wooden tea-light holders at either end for a relaxed touch.

Personal accents like wooden beads can tie the entire centerpiece together. For instance, I used them to curve gracefully around the arrangement, adding a charming and cohesive element.

This harmonious combination of colors, textures, and decor celebrates the beauty of spring while creating an inviting and elegant setting for your Mother's Day brunch.

Tablecloth

Choosing the right tablecloth for Mother's Day ensures you add a layer of sophistication to your table decor and will elevate the overall design. My favorite choices for this event are:

* **Solid tablecloths:** A solid hue in pale green, white, or pale violet will be a perfect base for your florals and vessels to create an elegant display where the arrangements are the star.
* **Patterned tablecloths:** Toile is a great choice for spring, since it gives off a light, airy feel and often features nature-inspired motifs, such as the bird theme on mine. A white and violet toile or a white and green toile tablecloth would be ideal for Mother's Day to tie in the season's colors.

Place Settings

Elegant place settings are the crowning touch in creating the classy, feminine atmosphere of this special brunch. Here's a list to create an irresistibly charming table:

1. Add your place mats. Round or patterned linen place mats in the color of your main scheme choice work the best. For instance, I used a sage-green round place mat to match my white and green tablecloth.
2. Mix and match plates. Your plates could have different colors or sizes or have various designs or patterns. The goal is that they create a bit of contrast while adding a cohesive touch to the table. I used a set of scalloped cream dinner plates, followed by sage-green side plates, and thrifted sage-green and white saucers with a silver rim.
3. Include small saucers and side plates for breads and butter.
4. Use champagne flutes and small wine glasses, which are perfect for ice water, orange juice, champagne, or wine. This adds to the elegance of your table.
5. Add a pocket napkin fold (see page 7). If you want to add a special touch, you can add a lilac blossom sprig inside the napkin.

LILAC-INFUSED SUGAR GIFTABLE

This craft is a beautiful and easy gift idea for your mother, or as a hostess gift. Lilac-infused sugar is simple to make and adds great flavor as a glass-rimmer or in baking. The sugar will last indefinitely, so feel free to let it sit longer than a week. The longer the sugar sits with the blossoms, the more potent the flavor will be.

1 cup (10 g) lilac blossoms and blooms, plucked or cut from the bases
1 small or medium container
1 sieve or mesh strainer, for removing flower bits
1½ cups (300 g) granulated sugar
3 small jam jars, for gifting
12-inch (30.5 cm) square burlap or fabric, for decorating the jar tops
3 elastics, for the jar tops
Jute twine, for the jar tops

1. Remove any green pieces from the bottom of the blossoms, then rinse the flowers in a colander and drain. Place the flowers on top of a paper towel and allow them to dry completely.

2. Press ½ cup (5 g) of lilac blossoms in a flower press or between two pages in a book. Set aside.

3. In a small or medium glass or plastic container, add a ½-inch (12 mm) to 1-inch (2.5 cm) layer of sugar, then a thin layer of lilacs. Repeat these layers until the container is full, leaving some room to shake up the contents. Cover the container with a paper towel and let it sit overnight.

4. The following day, put the lid on the container and shake up the contents for 5 seconds. Store the container in a cool, dark place, and shake up every 24 to 48 hours for at least 1 week before sifting.

5. Sift the sugar through a sieve or mesh strainer to remove flower bits before using.

6. Transfer the sifted lilac sugar into small jars and top them with a sprinkle of pressed lilacs.

7. Cut out burlap or fabric into 4-inch (10 cm) squares using scissors and secure them to the tops of the jars with an elastic band. Wrap jute twine around each elastic band a couple times and finish by tying a bow, like you would a shoelace, to create a charming presentation.

TIP

If you're in a hurry, you can chill the dough in the freezer for 30 minutes.

RECIPE

PERFECT PIECRUST

TOTAL TIME: 4 HOURS AND 15 MINUTES OR OVERNIGHT
YIELD: ONE APPROXIMATELY 12-INCH (30.5 CM) PIECRUST

This is the perfect piecrust for any recipe! Most piecrust recipes call for shortening, but in my experience, there is a far better alternative—butter! Yes, using butter will guarantee a delicious crust, but there is a catch! For the flakiest crust, freeze the butter and grate it with a cheese grater. This keeps the butter firm while you work the dough, creating perfectly flaky layers when the pie is baked.

1¼ cups (150 g) all-purpose flour, plus more for dusting
¼ teaspoon salt
½ cup (1 stick, or 115 g) unsalted butter, frozen
¼ cup (60 ml) ice-cold water

1. In a medium-sized bowl, whisk together the flour and salt. Using a coarse cheese grater, grate the frozen butter directly into the flour mixture. Frequently toss and combine the butter with the flour using a spatula, large spoon, or pastry cutter to prevent the butter shreds from sticking together.

2. Add the water slowly, working the dough with a spatula or your hands just enough for it to stick together. The dough will be hard. Form the dough into a disk, wrap it with plastic wrap, and place it in the refrigerator for at least 4 hours, or overnight.

3. Once chilled, place the dough on a well-floured surface. Roll it out gently from the center toward the edges, lifting the rolling pin at the end of each stroke rather than dragging it forward to avoid tearing. Rotate the dough 90 degrees after each roll. Lift and re-flour the surface as needed to prevent sticking. Continue until the dough forms a 10- to 12-inch (25 to 30.5 cm) circle. If you see visible butter shreds in your dough as you roll it out, this means you will have a fantastic crust

4. Transfer the dough to a 9-inch (23 cm) pie pan. Trim any excess or fold the edges under for a thicker crust. Prick the bottom and sides with a fork to prevent puffing. Press the fork around the edges for a decorative pattern. Chill the crust for 10 to 15 minutes to firm up the butter and reduce shrinkage.

5. To parbake or blind bake: Preheat the oven to 375°F (190°C). Place a large sheet of parchment paper into the empty pie shell and fill it with dried chickpeas or pie weights to prevent the crust from puffing up while baking. Bake for 10 to 12 minutes if parbaking, or 25 to 30 minutes if blind baking. Remove the chickpeas and parchment, then let the crust cool for 10 to 15 minutes before adding the filling. Continue baking until the filling is fully cooked; timing will vary depending on the type of filling.

NOTE

The type of filling you use in your pie will determine whether you blind-bake, par-bake, or don't bake the crust before adding the filling. Blind-baking fully cooks the crust for fillings that don't require baking (like cream fillings), par-baking partially cooks the crust for moderate-bake fillings (like custards and pumpkin pie), and no baking is used for longer-bake fruit pies (like apple and cherry pies).

GARDEN QUICHE

TOTAL TIME: 1 HOUR AND 10 MINUTES OR OVERNIGHT
YIELD: 8 TO 10 SERVINGS

This quiche recipe is sure to wow with its flavor and ease. If you're short on time, a store-bought piecrust is perfectly acceptable; however, I highly encourage you to make your own piecrust.

- 1 recipe Perfect Piecrust (see page 45)
- 6 eggs
- 1 ¼ cups (300 ml) heavy whipping cream
- 1 teaspoon salt
- 1 teaspoon black pepper
- ½ teaspoon cayenne pepper
- 1 cup (110 g) shredded mozzarella cheese
- ½ cup (60 g) crumbled feta cheese
- 1 cup (134 g) 1-inch (2.5 cm) asparagus chunks
- 8 to 10 whole asparagus spears, cut to varying lengths (from 3 to 7 inches, or 7.5 to 17 cm)
- ¼ cup (15 g) chopped green onions or chives

1. If using a homemade piecrust, follow the recipe on page 45 (steps 1 to 4), then preheat the oven to 375°F (190°C). Place a large sheet of parchment paper into the empty pie shell and fill it with dried chickpeas or pie weights to prevent the crust from puffing up while baking. Bake for 25 to 30 minutes for a blind bake. Remove the parchment paper and chickpeas or pie weights, then set aside to cool for 10 to 15 minutes. Reduce the oven heat to 350°F (175°C). If using a storebought piecrust, follow the instructions on the label.
2. In a medium bowl, add the eggs and whisk until they are thick and bubbly. Add the cream and whisk again. Stir in the salt, black pepper, cayenne pepper, and cheeses.
3. In the cooled piecrust, arrange 1-inch (2.5 cm) asparagus chunks where you plan to place the long asparagus spears on top. This will help support the spears and keep them visible on top of the quiche.
4. Pour the egg mixture over the piecrust. Place the asparagus spears over the asparagus chunks in the mixture, nudging, moving, and stacking any pieces as needed underneath the long spears to hold them up. Sprinkle green onion or chives over the mixture.
5. Carefully transfer the pan into the oven and bake for 30 minutes, or until the quiche is fully set. Serve warm and enjoy.

TIP

You can insert a knife into the center of the quiche to test if it's ready; if the knife comes out clean, it is done.

TIP

You can substitute feverfew blossoms with chamomile.

RECIPE

CRUDITÉS & FRUITS JALAPEÑO DIP BOARD

TOTAL TIME: 15 MINUTES **YIELD:** 8 TO 10 SERVINGS PLUS 2 CUPS (475 ML) OF DIP

You can elevate your typical mixed fruit and veggie platter by choosing more unique pairings and then slicing and arranging them in a gorgeous pattern. I like to group bright colors together and garnish with edible flowers for the perfect dainty spring vibe.

FOR THE JALAPEÑO DIP

1 to 2 large jalapeños, chopped finely
⅓ cup (15 g) fresh cilantro, roughly chopped
2 cloves garlic, crushed
1 medium lime
16 ounces (480 ml) sour cream
1 package (1 ounce, or 30 ml) ranch dressing mix
2 to 4 tablespoons 2% milk

FOR THE CRUDITÉS AND FRUITS

1 bunch fresh parsley
1 bunch carrot greens or herb sprigs of choice (optional)
2 large dark-yellow bell peppers
2 large light-yellow bell peppers or peppers of choice
1 cup (150 g) purple grape sprigs
1 cup (145 g) yellow cherry tomatoes or cherry tomatoes of choice
6 to 9 snap peas in the pod
10 edible feverfew blossoms or edible flower of choice
10 sprigs catmint or edible flower of choice

1. To make the jalapeño dip: In a food processor, add the jalapeños, cilantro, and garlic and pulse until finely chopped.
2. Cut the lime in half and squeeze the juice into the processor.
3. Add the sour cream and the ranch dressing mix into the processor and pulse until thoroughly combined.
4. Add the milk, 1 tablespoon at a time, into the processor until you reach a moderately thick dip-like consistency.
5. Add dip mixture to a serving bowl of your choice.
6. To make the Crudités and Fruits: Add the bowl of dip to the center of a circular board. Lay a base bed of parsley and any other greens around the bowl.
7. Slice the dark-yellow peppers thinly and place a grouping of 10 to 12 slices at the 4 o'clock, 8 o'clock, and 11 o'clock positions on your board.
8. Slice the light-yellow peppers or peppers of choice and place in groupings of 10 to 12 at the 2 o'clock, 7 o'clock, and 10 o'clock positions on the board.
9. Nestle in sprigs of purple grapes between the peppers.
10. Add clusters of yellow cherry tomatoes into remaining spaces.
11. Split snap peas open along their seam to remove half the shell and expose the cute peas in a pod; lay them out in groups of 3, side by side, or as you like on top.
12. Place edible flowers around the board over the veggies in a random pattern for the prettiest presentation.

TIPS

If you want to make this recipe ahead, you can prebake the sheet cake and wrap it well in plastic wrap and store it for up to 5 days. You can premake the frosting, cover, and refrigerate for up to 7 days. I do recommend whipping your frosting back up before piping. Tea cakes are best made fresh and served within a few hours but can be made a day ahead if necessary and stored in an airtight container. Also, feel free to use canola or vegetable oil instead of avocado oil.

BLUEBERRY TEA CAKES

RECIPE

TOTAL TIME: 50 MINUTES **YIELD:** 12 TO 15 TEA CAKES

These incredibly beautiful tea cakes will make you look like a professional baker. They look irresistible, and all your guests need to do is pop them on a plate!

FOR THE CAKES

3 cups (360 g) all-purpose flour
1 ¾ cups (350 g) granulated sugar
1½ teaspoons baking powder
1 teaspoon salt
4 large eggs
¾ cup (180 ml) avocado oil
1 cup (240 ml) whole or reduced-fat (2%) milk
1 tablespoon vanilla extract
Blueberries, for garnish
Mint leaves, for garnish

FOR THE FROSTING

1 cup (145 g) blueberries
½ cup (1 stick, or 115 g) unsalted butter, at room temperature
3 cups (360 g) confectioners' sugar, plus more as needed
1 teaspoon vanilla extract
1 tablespoon 2% milk

1. To make the cakes: Preheat the oven to 350°F (175°C) with a rack in the middle. Grease a 13 × 18-inch (33 × 46 cm) baking sheet with cooking spray. In a large mixing bowl or the bowl of a stand mixer, whisk the flour, sugar, baking powder, and salt together. Add the eggs, oil, milk, and vanilla, mixing on medium speed about 3 minutes, until smooth. Spread the batter evenly on the prepared baking sheet and place the baking sheet on the middle rack of your oven.

2. Bake for 20 to 25 minutes, until the cake is lightly browned and springs back when pressed. Let the cake cool on a wire rack for 5 to 10 minutes, then use a spatula to lift it away from the pan and slide it onto a wire rack to finish cooling.

3. To make the frosting: In a small saucepan, simmer the blueberries and 2 tablespoons of water over medium heat. Cook, stirring and mashing frequently, for 5 to 8 minutes, until rendered down and juicy. Strain the mixture into a bowl and set aside to cool.

4. In a large bowl or an electric hand mixer, beat the butter on medium speed until smooth. Add the confectioners' sugar ½ cup (60 g) at a time, beating well after each addition. Add the vanilla, milk, and 2 to 3 tablespoons of blueberry juice, beating until smooth and fluffy. Add more blueberry juice, a tablespoon at a time, to deepen the color and flavor as you like. If the mixture becomes too runny, add more confectioners' sugar. Whip the mixture for 5 to 8 minutes. You want to make sure that it is firm enough to hold its shape when piped.

5. Slide the sheet cake onto a cutting board. Use a 2 to 3-inch (5 to 7.5 cm) deep round cookie cutter or a greased round measuring cup to cut out 24 to 30 circles from the sheet cake.

6. Transfer the frosting into a piping bag fitted with a large star tip, and pipe the frosting onto a cake circle. Sandwich another cake circle on top, and pipe frosting on the top in a swirl. Garnish with blueberries and mint. Serve and enjoy!

RECIPE

LILAC GIN FIZZ COCKTAILS

TOTAL TIME: 8 HOURS AND 20 MINUTESS

YIELD: 4 SERVINGS PLUS 1 CUP (240 ML) OF LILAC SIMPLE SYRUP

Lilacs add the most beautiful and unique floral flavor, which you can use to bring the taste of spring into your drinks and desserts, such as this delicious cocktail that is sure to bring a festive smile to all who partake.

FOR THE LILAC SIMPLE SYRUP

1½ cups (15 g) lilac blossoms, rinsed (petals only, no green or it will be bitter)

2 to 3 frozen blueberries (optional)

½ cup (100 g) granulated sugar

FOR THE COCKTAILS

4 ounces (120 ml) gin

Juice of 1 large lemon

2 ounces (60 ml) Lilac Simple Syrup

10 ounces (300 ml) carbonated water, tonic, or Sprite, as preferred

12 to 20 blueberries

Ice cubes

1. To make the lilac simple syrup: In a small bowl, add the lilac blossoms and, if you'd like more of a purple color, the frozen blueberries.
2. In a small saucepan, stir together ½ cup (120 ml) of water and the sugar. Bring to a boil over medium-high heat, then turn off the heat and pour it over the lilac petals in the bowl. Allow the mixture to sit for 4 to 8 hours, or overnight. Strain the lilac blossoms and transfer the infused simple syrup to a jar.
3. To make the cocktails: Add the gin, lemon juice, simple syrup, and water, tonic, or Sprite to a pitcher and stir well.
4. Add 3 to 5 large blueberries and ice cubes to each cocktail glass.
5. Pour the mixture into the glasses and serve!

TIPS

You can keep the simple syrup in the refrigerator for up to 3 weeks or freeze in a mini–ice cube tray and store in a zip-top bag for up 3 months at peak freshness to have lilac flavor infusions all summer long! For the cocktails, add blueberries to the rim of the glasses and a sprig of mint if you'd like to coordinate beautifully with the other items on the Mother's Day menu! Also, you can omit the gin for a mocktail.

RAINY-DAY GAME NIGHT

Rainy spring days can be too wet, muddy, and often too cold to enjoy, but when there is nothing to be done outdoors, it can free up time to put together a special night and even start a memorable seasonal tradition for your family. Turning a low-key day into something special and totally out of the ordinary is the sort of thing that reminds us that there doesn't need to be any specific holiday or big family event happening for us to go all-out and make our everyday magical! Once the busyness of summer arrives, these nights are fewer and farther between, so I hope this fun idea inspires you to take a boring rainy day and add some creative kitchen time.

FUN & GAMES ON THE TABLE

A rainy day turned impromptu game night means less focus on fussy decor and more emphasis on fun. With just a few simple touches, you can create the perfect setting for friendly competition—complete with cozy vibes, easy ambiance, and delicious themed snacks.

The key to a great rainy-day game night is not overthinking it. The goal is to create a fun and thoughtful experience that feels spontaneous—without any stress. With a warm setting, easy setup, and simple yet festive food, you'll have the perfect recipe for bonding time with family filled with laughter, competition, and cozy memories.

Setting the Mood

To offset the dreary rainy-day atmosphere, start by creating warmth and comfort:

* Light a crackling fire in the fireplace or put on a fire channel on your smart TV.
* Scatter candles, twinkle lights, or lamps around the room for a soft glow.
* Bring out fuzzy blankets, extra pillows, and sheepskins for ultra-coziness.

With just these elements, you can transform a gloomy day into an inviting and relaxing game night setting.

Game-Night Table Setup

The game table should be functional yet fun. Set up a chessboard or favorite board game on a side table near your fireplace (if you have one), with ottomans or stacked cushions for seating. This instantly invites head-to-head competition.

For variety, have a secondary table ready with Scrabble, cards, or other favorite games, making it easy for players to switch between activities throughout the night.

Fun and Themed Finger Foods

No game night is complete without easy-to-grab snacks that double as decor. Try these ideas for a visually appealing and delicious spread:

* Gourmet pizza buns: easy to hold and eat mid-game
* Homemade trail mix: a customizable, no-mess snack
* Dice-shaped cookies: a fun, thematic touch
* Single-serve salads: a fresh and effortless addition

Serve everything on black tableware to make the colors pop, and nestle the food in alongside game pieces to keep everything feeling cohesive and interactive.

Other Fun Things to Consider

To enhance your rainy-day game night, a few extra touches can make the experience even more enjoyable.

* **Since drinks and games don't always mix well, you can opt for spillproof beverages to avoid accidents:**
    * Warm cider, hot chocolate, or tea in spillproof lidded mugs
    * Mini bottles of sparkling water or soda for easy sipping
    * Lots of napkins at the ready
* **Keep the game night running smoothly with a few handy extras:**
    * Small bowls for holding game pieces, dice, or tokens
    * Coasters and napkins to protect game boards and cards from spills
    * Pens and paper for keeping score
    * A speaker or device to play upbeat music and keep the energy high
* **Prizes:**
    * You may want to have some sweet treats or small prizes on hand for the big winners of the night

The Extra Mile

If you want to go the extra mile and make your rainy-day game night even more special, try adding these playful touches to your décor:

* Frame fun signage like "Let the Games Begin!" or "Rainy Day Fun"
* Use a small chalkboard or whiteboard to display the night's game lineup, team names, or scores
* Set out a bin or bowl filled with mystery mini-games or trivia questions for spontaneous fun
* Create DIY snack bars with themed stations—let guests build their own nachos, popcorn, fruit salad, or candy mix. Label each station with a playful name like "Candyland Corner," "Popcorn Poker," or "The Fruit Champs"
* Serve drinks in cute cups with game-themed name tags or stickers (if kids are attending, let them decorate their own cups!)
* Offer cozy socks or slippers for guests to wear throughout the night
* Set up a "Winner's Throne"—a decorated chair for the champion(s). This is especially fun for the little ones!

And if you're feeling extra creative, form teams for the night and give them cool, themed names to spark some friendly rivalry!

Take the time to experiment what works for you and your loved ones. Think about any games you'd like to try or love to play and make sure there is a little bit of everything for guests. Most of all, remember to enjoy yourself in the process.

SNACK MIX

MINI-DICE COOKIES

TOTAL TIME: 54 MINUTES **YIELD:** 40 TO 50 MINI COOKIES

These bite-size, buttery vanilla cookies topped with sweet frosting and chocolate are seriously addictive, along with being absolutely adorable. These cookies are the true stars of any game-day table.

FOR THE COOKIES

1½ cups (3 sticks, or 340 g) unsalted butter, at room temperature

1 cup (200 g) granulated sugar

1 teaspoon vanilla extract

3½ cups (420 g) all-purpose flour, plus more for dusting

¼ teaspoon salt

FOR THE ICING

3 large egg whites

½ teaspoon cream of tartar

3 to 4 cups (360 g to 480 g) confectioners' sugar

1 cup (185 g) mini chocolate chips

1. To make the cookies: Line two baking sheets with parchment paper and set aside. In the bowl of an electric mixer fitted with a paddle attachment, cream together the butter and sugar until just combined. Mix in the vanilla.
2. In a separate large mixing bowl, sift together the flour and salt, then combine with the butter mixture. Mix on low speed until the dough starts to come together. Transfer the dough onto a floured surface and bring it together with your hands.
3. Divide the dough into two equal pieces and flatten each into a 1-inch-thick (2.5 cm) rectangle. Cover and chill for 30 minutes. Preheat the oven to 350°F (175°C).
4. Place the dough between two large pieces of parchment paper and roll until you have a large, ¼-inch-thick (6 mm) rectangle. Using a straight-edge dough scraper, knife, or pizza cutter, cut the cookies into roughly 1-inch (2.5 cm) squares and place them on the prepared baking sheets about 2 inches apart (5 cm). Bake for 7 to 8 minutes, until the edges begin to turn golden. Remove to cool on a baking sheet.
5. To make the icing: In a stand mixer, whisk the egg whites on medium until light and fluffy. Add the cream of tartar and confectioners' sugar and mix on low until it reaches a toothpaste-like consistency. Be sure it's not too runny so it won't spread down your cookies. Transfer the icing to a piping bag fitted with a very narrow round tip.
6. Pipe a square around the inner perimeter of each cookie and fill it with icing. Press mini chocolate chips into the tops to create the dice patterns immediately after icing. Let the cookies set for 2 to 3 hours, until the icing is hard to the touch. Serve and enjoy.

TIPS

If you don't have a piping bag, you can dip the tops of the cookies in the icing and then remove, placing the icing side up on the baking rack. These cookies are great to add to the Roll-the-Dice Snack Mix on page 61.

ROLL-THE-DICE SNACK MIX

TOTAL TIME: 1 HOUR AND 10 MINUTES **YIELD:** 10 SERVINGS

Kick off your game-day spread with a homemade snack mix that will have your fingers deliciously salty all night. This is the kind of recipe you will make again and again.

3 cups (90 g) square-shaped cereal (such as Corn Chex)
3 cups (75 g) whole grain oats cereal (such as Cheerios)
3 cups (672 g) mini pretzels
3 cups (315 g) roasted peanuts
¾ cup (1½ sticks, or 170 g) salted butter, melted
¼ cup (60 ml) Worcestershire sauce
1 teaspoon seasoned salt
1 teaspoon garlic powder
½ teaspoon onion powder

1. Preheat the oven to 240°F (116°C).
2. In a very large bowl, combine the cereals, pretzels, and peanuts; mix them well and set aside.
3. In a small bowl, stir the butter, Worcestershire sauce, seasoned salt, garlic powder, and onion powder until well combined.
4. Pour the butter mixture over the top of the cereal mixture, turning and stirring well to coat evenly. Transfer to a Dutch oven or roasting pan.
5. Bake for 1 hour, stirring every 15 minutes. Turn off the oven.
6. Pour the mixture onto a parchment-lined baking sheet and return it to the oven. Allow it to dry completely as the oven cools for 1 hour.
7. Serve and enjoy!

TIP

You can enhance this snack mix recipe by adding the Mini-Dice Shortbread Cookies from page 59 for an extra touch of fun and deliciousness. Just make sure the snack mix is fully cooked and completely cooled before mixing in the charming cookies.

RECIPE

BAGUETTE PIZZA BUNANZA

TOTAL TIME: 25 TO 30 MINUTES **YIELD:** 12 SERVINGS

Get ready to raise the bar on open-faced pizza buns to gourmet status. This is a simple meal that once again gets the crowd going wild! The MVPs on this spread are fresh-from-the-bakery bread, and higher-quality gourmet toppings. Both are things you won't usually find on your average pizza sub, but I bet you won't be able to give them up now! Using my special technique of baking all the layers individually, you'll have a never-soggy, easy-to-hold-while-you-play food that feels like the perfect game-day addition.

- 2 fresh bakery baguettes
- 1 cup (55 g) sun-dried tomatoes
- 3½ ounces (100 g) deli smoked chicken, thinly sliced
- 3½ ounces (100 g) capocollo, thinly sliced
- 10 white mushrooms
- 2 to 3 mini red bell peppers
- 1 jar (12.3 ounces) gourmet pizza sauce
- 1 (12-ounce, or 340 g) mozzarella cheese ball, shredded
- ½ cup (20 g) fresh basil

1. Cut the ends off the baguettes, then cut the loaves into 3 equal pieces. Halve each piece horizontally to create 12 open-faced sandwich sides.
2. Thinly slice the sun-dried tomatoes, chicken, and capocollo into rectangular strips (about 2 to 3 inches long, or 5 to 7.5 cm). Set aside.
3. Slice the mushrooms straight down from their tops to give you perfect little mushroom-shaped slices. Slice the peppers into rounds. Set aside.
4. Preheat the oven to broil on medium setting. Spread 1 to 2 tablespoons of pizza sauce on each baguettes slice and broil until the sauce is dried, cooked, and the baguettes are toasted, about 3 to 4 minutes.
5. Add the chicken and capocollo slices, arranging them in horizontal lines on the pizza subs. You can add them together or make one of each variety. Broil again on the same setting for 2 to 3 minutes.
6. Add 1 to 2 tablespoons of shredded mozzarella on each, then place the tomato strips, peppers, mushrooms, and basil in a variety of combinations that look esthetically pleasing to you, like alternating horizontal lines of peppers and tomatoes, or all mushrooms in rows on the tops. Broil for 3 to 4 minutes, watching for the mozzarella to start to bubble and brown.
7. Allow the buns to cool for 3 to 4 minutes so the cheese sets up just a bit before serving!

TIP

You can make these pizzas 1 hour ahead and warm them up in the oven before serving, but they are best served fresh.

MINI CAESAR SALAD BITES

TOTAL TIME: 22 MINUTES **YIELD:** 12 CUPS

These pop-in-your-mouth, mini-size Caesar salad bites will have you winning compliments for best appetizer, even if you aren't winning card games. And the best part? The recipe only takes about 20 minutes to assemble.

- 2 cups (110 g) washed, dried, and finely chopped lettuce
- ¼ cup (60 ml) Caesar salad dressing
- ½ cup (20 g) croutons
- 2 cups (200 g) finely shredded Parmesan cheese
- Black pepper, to taste

1. In a medium bowl, wash and dry the lettuce, then chop it into extra fine pieces. Combine the lettuce with the Caesar salad dressing. Crush the croutons into coarse or fine crumbs (depending on your preference) by placing them in a resealable bag and pressing them with a rolling pin or the flat side of a heavy object. Place the crushed croutons in a separate bowl and set aside.
2. Preheat the oven to 350°F (175°C) and line a baking sheet with parchment paper. Set out an upside-down mini muffin tin nearby so it's ready for shaping the Parmesan cups quickly in Step 4.
3. Spoon mounds of 1 ½ tablespoons of Parmesan cheese on the prepared baking sheet, and use the spoon or your fingers to spread the mounds into 2- to 3-inch (5 to 7.5 cm) circles. Bake for 4 minutes and then allow them to cool on the pan for 1 minute.
4. Using a thin metal spatula or pie serving utensil, quickly transfer the Parmesan disks onto the protruding bowl shapes on the upside-down mini-muffin tin. Put the pan back into the oven for 1 minute to allow the cheese to melt into the cup shapes. Let them cool on the muffin tin.
5. Arrange the Parmesan cups on a serving platter and add the salad into each one. Sprinkle with the crushed croutons and a bit of pepper.
6. Serve and enjoy!

FATHER'S DAY FIESTA

To me, Father's Day is the trickiest event to set up in a masculine way that both honors the dads in the way they would like to be wined and dined on their day, and feels beautifully styled for entertaining with family and photographing. Well, enter the Father's Day Fiesta theme, and problem solved! With a Southwest flair carrying all the way through the table, food, and drinks, this is a theme that everyone can enjoy and have so much fun with. The late spring accents all fit together so beautifully in a way that makes every detail work, right down to the gifts (a Father's Day bouquet that's all about him). This is a theme that's so loved by all that it's easy to make it a Father's Day tradition from year to year!

A TOAST TO DAD

Crafting a fun, fiesta-themed Father's Day tablescape is the perfect way to celebrate the dads in our lives with style and flair. This special setup combines masculine elements with tasteful, seasonal touches, creating an inviting and memorable atmosphere for both dining and family photos. The following sections break down how you can create your own fiesta-inspired Father's Day table.

Florals and Colors

While flowers may not be the first thing that comes to mind for Father's Day, they can make a great addition to a family gathering when styled in a casual, unfussy way that dads can appreciate. For my table, I chose vibrant yellow tones and relaxed greenery to create a cheerful yet laid-back atmosphere. Here are my floral recommendations to create this dad-filled fiesta day:

* **Yellow, orange, or red marigolds:** Native to Mexico, these late-spring blooms add vibrant color and festive energy, symbolizing the sun and honoring the head of the family.
* **Yellow or orange alstroemeria:** Affordable and long-lasting, these bright blooms represent strength and devotion, perfect for celebrating dads.
* **Yellow, green, or red asters:** Easy to find and full of warmth, they symbolize happiness and good fortune.
* **Greenery:** Carrot greens, parsley, cilantro, or foraged leafy stems add a casual, fresh vibe to the arrangement.

These floral choices strike the perfect balance between festive and masculine. Don't be afraid to mix and match—just keep the palette warm and inviting.

Centerpieces and Decor Suggestions

For my tablescape, the centerpiece was the main attraction—a yellow marigold floral arrangement with some small touches of neutral colors throughout. You don't have to use yellow flowers, but if you do opt for the floral arrangement to take center stage, the following colors work great to keep it all looking cohesive:

* **Dark hues:** Add small touches of black to make the vibrant yellows pop, such as black plates.
* **White or neutral tones:** Use these colors for table linens or dishes for a clean and balanced look.

For a dramatic, long, and low masculine centerpiece, try using two rectangular plastic flower vessels with lids, like the ones available on Amazon, placed end to end for added impact. Alternatively, you can use any long vessels or even a row of shallow bowls. Fit them with crumpled chicken wire to securely hold your flowers and greenery in place.

For candles, keep the mood relaxed by adding:

* Wooden tea light holders for a natural touch
* Bright candle holders in primary colors for a playful vibe
* Glass tea light holders for an elegant finish

To enhance your table, include small plates or platters at each end of the centerpiece. Decorative green leaf plates, for example, work wonderfully to hold limes or mini bowls of sour cream, salsa, and hot sauce during dinner, adding both charm and functionality.

Tablecloth

For my Father's Day table, I opted for a bold-striped tablecloth in tan and white and layered it with a smaller-striped table runner in beige and white. But other ideal options for this theme are:

* **Solid tablecloth:** To keep with the fiesta vibe, I would opt for rich and bold hues like red, yellow, green, or blue to add to this playful theme.
* **Patterned tablecloth:** A fun bold stripe, as I used on my table, in a tan, yellow, or bright bold hue would match the mood well.
* **Table runners:** Any contrasting table runner in a complementary bold color or neutral tone (white, cream, tan) will create separation and drama for the centerpiece.

The right tablecloth acts as a canvas for your fiesta theme. Choose one that complements your florals and decor, and don't be afraid to layer textures for added depth and personality.

Place Settings

Create a bold and inviting table setting with the following easy steps:

* Start with bright, bold place mats that coordinate with your chosen Southwest color palette.
* Add a neutral- or secondary-colored napkin to tie the look together.
* Use layered plates—combine a bright and dark option to create striking contrast. For example, pair a deep-green dinner plate with a white side plate and a sage-green saucer with a white center and silver rim for a cohesive yet dynamic look.
* Finish with simple glassware—perfect for water or wine, leaving plenty of room for festive drinks like margaritas or Coronas.

This setup is easy to recreate and will leave your table looking effortlessly stylish and ready for celebration! By combining bold colors with clean lines and layered textures, your place settings will echo the spirit of the entire tablescape—fun, relaxed, and full of personality. Whether you're hosting an outdoor or an indoor dinner, these details help each guest feel welcomed and celebrated, especially the dads at the heart of it all.

OH HENRY!
Titleist
#1 ball in golf
Extra
PRO V1X
DAD
JOKES
—BREWED FRESH DAILY—

A FATHER'S DAY GIFT BOUQUET

We all know bouquets are a go-to for Mother's Day, but dads deserve to be treated to a thoughtful, esthetic gift too, and this is where the dad-approved "favorite things" mixed bouquet takes center stage! This thoughtful and fun gift can be made on a small budget and will show Dad how much he is loved.

- 1 large foam ball
- 1 large dad-themed mug
- 12 to 18 inches (30 to 45 cm) wooden dowels (⅜ to ½ inch, or 9.5 to 12.7 mm thick—thick enough to hold up a beer or golf balls)
- Tape
- Wooden skewers
- All Dad's favorite little things (such as candies, sporting event tickets, beers, boxes of golf balls, etc.)
- 2 (20-piece) packages of gift tissue paper (such as one gold and one black)
- 2 meters/yards jute twine or any string
- Fresh or faux flowers

1. Cut the foam ball to fit snugly into a dad-themed mug; insert it into the mug to create the base.
2. Tape all of Dad's favorite things to the wooden dowels or skewers, securing them into the foam.
3. Arrange the items in the foam, then fill out the arrangement with tissue paper "poms" or "flowers" added to the skewers.
4. To make tissue flowers: Stack 4 to 5 sheets of 12-inch (30.5 cm) square tissue paper and accordion-fold them 1 inch (2.5 cm) at a time. Secure the center with jute twine or string, then peel apart the layers to create a flower.
5. Attach the tissue flowers to skewers with tape and insert them around the gifts.
6. Add flowers (such as large garden marigolds) or dollar-store faux flowers for extra decoration.

RECIPE

FLOUR TORTILLAS

TOTAL TIME: 48 MINUTES **YIELD:** 8 TORTILLAS

These super-simple flour tortillas are significantly superior in both taste and texture to store-bought ones, and they are a big cost savings. I like to double this recipe and freeze half for later. This recipe is great to use when making the Butternut Squash Enchiladas on page 75.

- 1½ cups (180 g) all-purpose flour, plus more for dusting
- ½ teaspoon salt
- 1½ teaspoons baking powder
- 3 tablespoons avocado oil
- ½ cup (120 ml) warm water

1. Prepare a large plate with a large piece of tin foil or clean flour-sack towel on it and set aside.
2. In a large bowl, combine the flour, salt, and baking powder and whisk well.
3. In a separate small bowl, combine the avocado oil and water. Add the liquid to the dry ingredients ¼ cup (60 ml) at a time and mix until well combined.
4. Transfer the dough onto a lightly floured work surface. Knead until it's smooth and soft, about 3 minutes. Cut the dough into 8 equal pieces, then roll the pieces into smooth balls.
5. Cover the dough balls with a damp flour-sack towel or a damp paper towel. Let them rest for 20 minutes at room temperature to allow the gluten chains in the dough to relax, making the dough easier to roll.
6. On a lightly floured surface, roll out a ball of dough until it's very thin, under ⅛ inch (3 mm), and 6 inches in diameter (15 cm).
7. Heat a large stainless-steel or cast-iron skillet over medium-low heat. Cook a tortilla for 1 to 2 minutes on one side, until the bottom has golden brown spots and the top starts to bubble, puffing up. Flip the tortilla and cook for another 30 seconds, or until you start to see golden spots.
8. Transfer the tortilla onto the prepared plate lined with tin foil or a clean flour-sack towel and lay another piece of foil over the top. Fold the edges to keep the heat in. Repeat the cooking and covering process with your remaining dough, stacking up the tortillas. Keep your tortillas covered until you're ready to use them to prevent them from drying out.

TIP

Tortillas are best served fresh and warm, but can be frozen in a zip-top freezer bag and used later.

TIPS

If you want to add more protein, add shredded chicken. You can also cook the topping sauce at the same time that you are making the filling to save on time. Also, instead of using jarred salsa, you can make your own with the Fresh & Fab Five-Minute Salsa recipe on page 77.

BUTTERNUT SQUASH ENCHILADAS

TOTAL TIME: 1 HOUR AND 20 MINUTES **YIELD:** 16 ENCHILADAS

This recipe is one of our family favorites and has always been a huge hit with my husband, making it an easy go-to for this fiesta. This recipe will yield enough for two batches of eight enchiladas, and I always freeze half for later use, making this a win-win every time I make it.

FOR THE FILLING

1 medium butternut squash
¼ cup (½ stick, or 55 g) salted butter, divided
1 medium red onion, diced
2 cups (480 ml) jarred salsa of choice
1 teaspoon ground cumin
1 teaspoon cayenne pepper (optional)
1 teaspoon chili powder
1 teaspoon curry powder
1 teaspoon ground turmeric (optional)
1 can (15.25 ounces, or 432 g) corn, drained
1 can (15.5 ounces, or 439 g) black beans, drained and rinsed
8 Flour Tortillas (see page 73)
2 cups (230 g) shredded cheddar cheese, divided

FOR THE SAUCE

1½ cups (12 ounces, or 340 g) jarred salsa of choice
¼ cup (60 ml) heavy cream or whole milk
½ teaspoon chili powder
½ teaspoon curry powder
Sour cream, for serving (optional)
Hot sauce, for serving (optional)
Diced chives for serving (optional)
Green onions, for serving (optional)

1. To make the filling: Peel the squash and remove ends. Cut it in half lengthwise, and scoop out the seeds. Cut the squash into ½-inch (12 mm) cubes. In a large sauté pan, heat half of the butter over medium heat. Add the squash and sauté until it starts to brown and soften, about 10 minutes. Add the onions and remaining butter to the pan. Continue sautéing until the onions turn translucent and slightly brown, 3 to 4 minutes.
2. Add the salsa, cumin, cayenne pepper (if using), chili powder, curry powder, and turmeric (if using) and combine well. Add the corn and beans. Cook on medium-low heat for 5 to 10 minutes, until the beans and corn have softened and all the flavors have combined. Remove from the heat.
3. To make the enchilada sauce: In a small saucepan, combine the salsa, cream or milk, chili powder, and curry powder and cook on medium-low heat, stirring frequently until the sauce becomes thick. Remove from the heat once it's at the right consistency.
4. Preheat the oven to 350°F (175°C).
5. Fill each tortilla with about ½ cup to ¾ cup (120 to 180 ml) of the filling and 2 tablespoons cheese. Roll the tortillas and place in a rectangular or square baking dish. Spread the enchilada sauce across all the enchiladas and top with the remaining cheese.
6. Bake for 20 minutes, or until the toppings are bubbly and golden.
7. Serve with optional sour cream, hot sauce, and diced chives or green onions.

RECIPE

FRESH & FAB FIVE-MINUTE SALSA

TOTAL TIME: 5 MINUTES **YIELD:** 3 TO 4 CUPS (720 TO 960 ML)

This salsa is a tortilla-chip game changer, especially when made with a variety of fresh and delicious hothouse or garden tomatoes. The fact that this salsa comes together in a food processor in under five minutes with extremely minimal prep work (and that it can be made with canned diced tomatoes, too) makes it a recipe you will come back to again and again. It's guaranteed to become a staple once you try it!

4 cloves garlic, peeled and cut in half
1 large red onion, coarsely chopped
½ jalapeño pepper, seeds removed
6 large fresh tomatoes, cut into quarters
2 teaspoons sea salt
½ cup (25 g) roughly chopped fresh parsley
1 cup (40 g) roughly chopped fresh cilantro

1. In a food processor, add the garlic and onion and pulse 2 to 3 times for 2 to 3 seconds.
2. Add the jalapeño and pulse 2 to 3 times again.
3. Add the tomatoes and pulse 2 to 3 more times.
4. Add the salt, parsley, and cilantro and pulse 2 to 3 times for 2 to 3 seconds, scraping down the sides, until it's coarsely mixed.
5. Pour the salsa into a medium bowl and serve.

TIPS

If you can, include a mixed variety of tomatoes like Romas and slicers. You can also substitute the tomatoes for a can of diced tomatoes. If your ingredients are less fresh (hello winter produce!) or if your salsa is thick, add a splash or two of olive oil and red wine vinegar, then pulse once or twice. This will bring out the flavors and add just the right touch!

HOT JALAPEÑO CHEESY SKILLET CORN

TOTAL TIME: 35 MINUTES **YIELD:** 4 TO 6 SERVINGS

This splendidly spicy cheesy skillet corn is a quick and easy dish that pairs perfectly with tacos, nachos, or enchiladas as a side. It can even be turned into a main dish by serving over rotini or penne pasta! It also stores beautifully in the fridge overnight as a make-ahead dish.

2 tablespoons salted butter
1 small red onion, finely chopped
2 to 3 cloves garlic, crushed
4 cups (540 g) frozen corn
2 large jalapeños, seeds removed, diced
½ cup (120 ml) heavy cream
½ cup (115 g) cream cheese
1 cup (115 g) shredded white cheddar cheese
¼ cup (10 g) coarsely chopped fresh cilantro, for garnish
Lime wedges, for garnish

1. In a medium skillet, melt the butter over medium heat. Add the onions and sauté for 3 minutes, or until they start to become transparent. Stir n the garlic and cook for 1 minute.
2. Add the corn and stir well, cooking for 3 minutes. Add the jalapeños. Cook for 5 to 7 minutes, stirring frequently and letting any water evaporate.
3. Add the cream and cream cheese, stirring until well combined. When it thickens up, remove from the heat and add the cheddar cheese, stirring until melted.
4. Garnish with cilantro and lime wedges.

SLUSH-IN-A-RUSH LIMEADE MARGARITAS

TOTAL TIME: 5 MINUTES **YIELD:** 4 SERVINGS

I love this margarita recipe because it's fun and easy to make, using the can the limeade comes in as your only measuring tool! It only has four ingredients, none of the additives the pricey mixes have—and best of all, it's consistently delicious!

1 can (12 ounces, or 355 ml) frozen limeade concentrate
¼ can (3 ounces, or 90 ml) orange-flavored liqueur (such as Triple Sec)
¾ can (9 ounces, or 266 ml) tequila
2 cans (24 ounces) ice
Coarse salt, for rim
1 medium lime, sliced, for rim and garnish

1. In a high-power blender, add the frozen limeade concentrate, orange-flavored liqueur, tequila, and ice and blend until it is a slushy texture.
2. Pour a ¼-inch (6 mm) depth of salt into a small bowl or dish. Slide a lime wedge around the rim of each glass, then turn the glasses upside down and twist them in the salt to coat the rims.
3. Pour the margarita slush into the glasses and garnish with a lime slice. Enjoy!

SUMMER

One day, you find yourself on your deck with a glass of wine, the sounds of children playing outdoors, and you just know: Summer is here. This season's taste is all about fresh tomatoes, crisp greens, berries, citrus over ice, and smoky grill flavors shared outdoors with loved ones. Summer is a vibrant kaleidoscope of color and life. Strawberry reds, petal pinks, citrus oranges, and a yellow sun in an azure-blue sky, set against green grass. Nature's celebration is everywhere, from insects to flowers. Let this inspire your gatherings in the sweet summer heat.

PICNIC IN THE SUN

A beautiful summer afternoon deserves to be romanticized, and nothing says romanticized summer better than a perfectly planned and adorably styled picnic. There's just something magical about laying a blanket in a grassy spot under dappled sunlight, enjoying one of life's simple seasonal pleasures with one (or a few!) of your favorite people alongside a cute table and a delicious spread. While this is not a traditional table setup, there is no fun in summer without a picnic feast, so in this section, I will give my tips for setting up a picnic for you and some of your favorite people.

After all, the summer is not complete without at least one creative spread outside. It's also a great opportunity to connect with nature while enjoying a nice meal with the ones you love most.

TEA FOR TWO PICNIC

Though a picnic can be as simple as a sandwich on a blanket with the sun on your face and a breeze on your back, if you want to elevate the experience, there are a few key items that I recommend, which I've broken down in the following sections. Before we get into the essentials, let's talk styling first.

Styling

For styling, you can use your chosen food and surroundings as the color inspirations. For instance, you can carry the bright yellow of a custard, the vibrant red of berries, or the rich green of the summer grass theme up to your tabletop. I used a berry-themed tea towel, bright-green side plates, a fun lemon pitcher, and berry-colored, swoon-worthy dahlias to make my tabletop simply feel like summer.

Table

The first item you'll need for a picnic is a low table. You can create one yourself simply by using a couple of milk crates or cinderblocks a few feet apart with a few boards running lengthwise, which you'll cover with a tablecloth, or you can add a portable picnic table to your collection. I love the ease of knowing I can be picnic-ready anywhere, anytime, with this fun accessory!

Cushions

I love having a couple cushions to sit on for essential bottom comfort, and then also adding extras to stack on if eating. I used two inexpensive round seat cushions that I cut the ties off of for my tea party picnic, but you can be liberal with how many cushions you use to create the ideal feel.

Blanket

Laying out a picnic blanket goes without saying. Depending on your location, you may want to add a waterproof base layer; to do that, you can use a waterproof plastic tablecloth or drop cloth typically found at many dollar stores. You can also choose to use an outdoor rug as your designated picnic perch! There are so many options and ways to get creative with your base layer. For instance, here I simply used a large gingham tablecloth to create the perfect base.

Basket

To complete your picnic scene, you need a picnic basket (naturally). Generally made of wicker or rattan, they're often available at local retailers all through the spring. I found my own wicker picnic baskets secondhand, so I recommend checking online secondhand marketplaces, thrift stores, and garage sales. The perfect woven picnic basket will add rustic charm to your picnic setup, and you can use it throughout the years.

Herbs

SUMMER HERB PLANTER

A great summer herbal craft to keep the flavors of the season alive through the end of the year and even year-round is to create an indoor herb planter to place in a window in your home. There are many great cooking herbs that can easily be grown indoors, including chives, mint, parsley, basil, rosemary, cilantro, thyme, and oregano. I recommend using a pot with proper drainage to prevent waterlogging and a tray or cachepot to catch excess water and keep your windowsill clean. Growing the herbs for your herb planter can be done a few ways, which I've detailed below.

Herb seeds, cut stems, or fresh herbs
Soil, if growing from seed
Pot with drainage
Tray or cachepot

GROWING FROM SEED

1. Place herb seeds into soil in a pot.
2. Set the pot in a sunny window and water regularly (about one or two times per week).

GROWING FROM CUTTINGS

1. Cut stems from fresh herbs or buy fresh herbs from the grocery store.
2. Remove the bottom leaves and place the stems in water or soil.
3. Set the container in a sunny window and wait for roots to grow.
4. If rooting in water, change the water every 2 to 3 days.
5. Transfer rooted cuttings to a pot with soil. Set the pot in a sunny window and water regularly (about one or two times per week).

REPOTTING EXISTING HERBS

1. Buy new herbs from a garden center or dig up herbs from your garden, making sure to include lots of roots.
2. Transplant the herbs into a pot or multi-section herb planter.
3. Place the planter in a sunny window and water regularly (about one or two times per week).

RECIPE

MARVELOUS MINI PAVLOVAS

TOTAL TIME: 2 HOURS 15 MINUTES **YIELD:** 10 TO 12 MINI PAVLOVA MERINGUES

Pavlova meringues are a beautiful vessel for delicious fresh summer fillings, making them the perfect addition to a pretty picnic spread. They look deceivingly complex with their delicate, piped look, but despite being so impressive, they couldn't be easier to make!

4 large egg whites
1 cup (200 g) caster or granulated sugar
½ teaspoon cream of tartar
1½ teaspoons cornstarch
2 teaspoons vanilla extract
Whipped cream, for topping (optional)
Berries, for topping (optional)

1. Preheat the oven to 320°F (160°C). Line two baking sheets with parchment paper.
2. In a large, dry mixing bowl or the bowl of a stand mixer, beat the egg whites on high speed until soft peaks form.
3. Slowly add a couple of tablespoons of sugar at a time to the bowl while mixing, allowing it to dissolve into the egg whites. Add the cream of tartar and keep beating at high speed. Add the cornstarch and vanilla. Beat until stiff peaks form.
4. Place the meringue in a piping bag fitted with a large star tip. Pipe it onto the prepared baking sheets by creating 10 to 12 circles, swirling the meringue from the inside out, overlapping the outer edges of each circle once or twice to create a deep well. If you don't want to pipe these, you can spoon 10 to 12 dollops onto the baking sheet and scoop out the center or press a spoon into the center to create a well.
5. Put the baking sheets in the oven and right away lower the temperature to 245°F (120°C).
6. Bake for 30 minutes, then lower the temperature again to 200°F (90°C).
7. Bake for an additional 30 minutes, until the meringues feel dry when lightly touched.
8. Turn off the oven and open the oven door a few inches, leaving the meringues inside to finish cooling more slowly. This will ensure that your meringues do not crack as they finish drying.
9. Add whipped cream and fresh berries to the top, if desired, and serve!

TIP

The Coconut Custard (see page 91) and Raspberry Simple Syrup and Compote (see page 93) recipes make the perfect toppings for the pavlovas.

COCONUT CUSTARD

TOTAL TIME: 30 MINUTES **YIELD:** 2 CUPS (480 ML)

This delicious custard makes the perfect topping for all sorts of tarts and desserts, and the best things is that you can use it on are the Marvelous Mini Pavlovas on page 89. The key to excellent, smooth custard is stirring your way through all the steps.

¼ cup (50 g) granulated sugar
3 large egg yolks
2 tablespoons all-purpose flour
1 teaspoon cornstarch
Pinch of salt
¾ cup (180 ml) canned coconut cream
½ teaspoon vanilla extract

1. In a medium mixing bowl, stir together the sugar and egg yolks until all the sugar has dissolved and the mixture is pale yellow and runny. Add the flour, cornstarch, and salt to the bowl and mix completely. Set aside.
2. In a small saucepan, heat the coconut cream on low heat, stirring occasionally to prevent a film from forming. Warm until bubbles appear at the edges, but do not let it boil. The goal is to make it very warm.
3. Very slowly add the coconut cream to the egg yolk mixture, stirring continuously. Pouring too quickly can result in the egg yolks becoming scrambled, so easy does it!
4. Once the mixture is completely combined, return it to the saucepan and cook on medium to low heat, stirring to avoid lumps from forming. Add the vanilla and continue stirring for 5 to 15 minutes, until it thickens. Once you see the mixture start to thicken, remove from the heat. If there are lumps, pour the mixture through a mesh strainer to remove/resolve the lumps.
5. Transfer the custard to a container with a lid, leaving the lid slightly open to allow it to cool down without drying out. Once cooled, enjoy as is or refrigerate for a few hours!

TIP

This custard can be kept in the fridge for 3 to 4 days. Chilling the custard will create a thicker consistency.

RASPBERRY MINT GREEN TEA

TOTAL TIME: 21 MINUTES

YIELD: 4 CUPS (960 ML) PLUS ½ TO ¾ CUP (120 TO 180 ML) OF SIMPLE SYRUP

The ideal complement to your picnic is a delicious tea—light, fruity, and infused with minty green goodness. Even better, the Raspberry Simple Syrup used in the tea doubles as a compote, making it a perfect topping for the Marvelous Mini Pavlovas recipe on page 89.

FOR THE RASPBERRY SIMPLE SYRUP

½ cup (100 g) granulated sugar

1 cup (125 g) fresh raspberries

FOR THE MINT GREEN TEA

2 ounces (60 ml) Raspberry Simple Syrup

2 green-tea bags

½ cup (25 g) fresh mint

1. To make the simple syrup: In a small saucepan, stir together ½ cup (120 ml) of water, the sugar, and raspberries. Bring to a boil, then reduce to a high simmer, stirring frequently for 3 to 5 minutes, until the raspberries start to melt into the liquid. Strain the simple syrup (see Note) through a mesh sieve, pouring the liquid into a small jar.
2. To make the mint green tea: Bring 4 cups (960 ml) of water to a boil. In a glass teapot fitted with a tea infuser, add the simple syrup, tea bags, and fresh mint to the infuser, and then the boiling water. Steep for 4 minutes before drinking, and enjoy.

NOTE

The raspberry compote is made from the solids left behind after straining the simple syrup. Simply transfer the strained raspberries to a small dish and serve as a sweet, fruity topping.

Lara

AL FRESCO DINNER

Although the term al fresco originates from Italy, meaning "in the cool" or "in the fresh," the use of al fresco to describe relaxed outdoor dining is more of an English or American adaptation than Italian, believe it or not! It became popular in the mid-twentieth century, and over time, this romantic-sounding title, feeling more upscale than simply "eating outside," had spread around the world.

For me, al fresco dining means that nature becomes the sights and sounds of the dining room. When the weather is right, there is no need for music or screens to add to the ambiance. The scents of the garden, the sounds of the breeze in the trees, the beautiful flowers in bloom, and all the calm activity of nature around us serve as the perfect dinner music and entertainment for all five senses.

Every bite is savored alongside the beauty of the world outside.

AN OPEN-AIR AFFAIR

An al fresco setting provides you with a unique opportunity to embrace the beauty of nature while having an elevated dining experience. It allows you to blend your personal style with the wonders of the natural world, from the tallest of trees to the smallest of flowers. To achieve an elegant yet relaxed look, suitable for a sundress-and-shorts dinner, I like using blue as the base color to mirror the summer sky and contrast with the greens of nature. Here are my suggestions on creating your very own al fresco experience.

Florals

The following are my recommendations of flowers that are in season and pair beautifully with a blue-based outdoor summer scene:

* **Bachelor's buttons:** These flowers are pretty, frilly, and come in bright blue, light blue, and pastel pinks and purples.
* **Sweet peas:** These flowers are sweetly scented summer favorites and frequently come in deep and light blues, reds, and whites.
* **Blue salvia:** These pretty deep-blue blossoms have a lovely scent and grow on tall and plentiful spikes.
* **Snapdragons:** Another spike-type floral that is available in abundance during the summer and comes in a rainbow of bright and light colors; they pair perfectly with all the other flowers in this list.

Colors

Creating a table setup that stands out yet complements the garden scene can be tricky, especially if you're like me and love green. As mentioned before, blue is ideal for this type of setting, as it stands out without being overwhelming. So, it goes without saying that I recommend using blue as a main color for this setup along with white. Some blue hues and other complementary tones that work great include:

* **Navy:** A deep blue that pairs beautifully with other blues, whites, creams, or bright yellow and creates a sophisticated and fresh summer look.
* **Light blue:** Light blue lends itself to whites as well, along with soft, summer pinks and soft butter yellow for a pretty and light garden-party vibe.
* **Royal blue:** Brings a fun summer party palette paired with hot pink or bright red, and looks great with whites too.
* **Turquoise:** Creates a tropical mood when you add warm-toned yellows, corals, and pinks.

If blue is not your preferred color, you can use the following alternate colors:

* Dusty rose
* Blush pink
* Coral
* Amber
* Marigold

These colors add warmth to the summer scene without clashing with nature or being too overwhelming.

Centerpieces and Decor Suggestions

Adding a few natural elements on your table gives it a polished look without feeling overdone. Wood candleholders and burlap table runners are great examples of pieces you can use to give your table a laid-back touch.

Using natural elements creates a relaxed outdoor mood that can carry forward into the food. Here are a few more ideas:

* **Long, low arrangements:** Use shallow bowls or a row of rectangular vessels. Line them with crumpled chicken wire or floral foam to securely hold your flowers, creating a relaxed yet elegant display.
* **Functional decor:** Include small serving bowls or platters at each end of the centerpiece to hold snacks or condiments, subtly blending functionality with charm.

Adding thoughtful centerpieces, such as low arrangements or functional decor, will help you create an inviting and polished outdoor table setting.

Tablecloth

For my al fresco scene, I added a light-blue striped tablecloth as my grounding layer under a navy blue and white umbrella. But you could also use:

* A solid tablecloth in navy, bright blue, or a crisp white or light cream. These colors also stand out well in a grassy green or garden scene.
* A patterned tablecloth such as an elegant floral pattern with light blues and navy, or a tropical pattern with turquoise and corals. A blue and white stripe or a light blue on white polka dot would also be lovely.

Whether solid color or patterned, the tablecloth will set the foundation for your al fresco decor, connecting elegance with the beauty of the outdoors.

Place Settings and Chairs

I recommend keeping the color theme you've chosen cohesive and repeating throughout your setup with various coordinating pieces. From the plates, vases, and napkins, all the way to the chairs or coordinating chair cushions if you have them.

I repeated the blue theme throughout my table decor with blue-seated bentwood chairs, blue plates and vases, and blue-and-white striped napkins. Then, for the perfect monochromatic touch, I opted to use blue salvia as my floral accent.

Lara

HERB BOUQUET PLACE MARKERS

A special and thoughtful addition to an al fresco table is these mini-vase place markers that you can fill with variety of fresh herbs. It also makes for a great gift!

A variety of fresh herb sprigs of choice
Jute twine
Printer or pen
Card stock
Scissors
Hot glue
Hot glue gun
Skewers
Mini vases, bud vases, or small jars

1. Gather little bundles of mixed herbs (such as parsley, rosemary, mint, thyme, and oregano) together, and secure with a piece of jute twine.
2. Print or write the names of your guests on card stock. Cut the card stock into little tags, using the scissors to make fun shapes, and hot-glue them onto the skewers.
3. Add the herbs and some water to all the vases. Place the name-tag skewers into the vases and transfer them to your table setting.

TIPS

The best part is that you can send your guests home with the little herbal bundles to hang to dry or use fresh in their own kitchens. If you use small vases that you don't wish to keep, you can also gift the entire vases.

RECIPE

GRISSINI BREADSTICKS

TOTAL TIME: 1 HOUR AND 45 MINUTES **YIELD:** 24 TO 30 STICKS

These crunchy Italian breadsticks paired with a trio of whipped feta dips (page 102) make the absolute perfect al fresco appetizer or side dish. The only problem is making sure your guests don't fill up on them before the main course!

- ½ cup (75 g) sesame seeds
- 3 ⅓ cups (450 g) bread flour, plus more for dusting
- 1 teaspoon honey
- 1½ teaspoons instant yeast
- 2 teaspoons salt
- 1 cup plus 3 tablespoons (285 ml) warm water
- ¼ cup (60 ml) extra-virgin olive oil, plus a little more for brushing

1. Preheat the oven to 350°F (175°C). Line a baking sheet with parchment paper.
2. Spread the sesame seeds evenly on the baking sheet and toast them in the oven, shaking the sheet every couple of minutes, until golden brown, about 5 to 10 minutes. Set aside.
3. In the bowl of a stand mixer fitted with dough hook, or in a large bowl with a hand mixer, combine the flour, honey, and yeast. Stir on low speed and then add the salt. Gradually add the warm water while mixing, followed by the olive oil. Continue mixing until the dough comes together, then knead on low speed for 3 to 4 minutes.
4. Transfer the dough to a lightly floured surface and shape it into an oblong log. Cover with a tea towel or flour-sack towel and let rest for 12 minutes.
5. Roll the dough out to a ½-inch-thick (12 mm), 20 × 5-inch (50 × 12 cm) wide rectangle. Brush the top with olive oil and lightly dust with flour. Using a dough scraper, flip the dough over and brush the other side with olive oil. Coat generously with the toasted sesame seeds, pressing them in lightly. Dust with a little more flour.
6. Cover the dough with plastic wrap and a linen towel and let it rest at room temperature for 1 hour.
7. Preheat the oven to 400°F (205°C). Using a dough cutter or pizza cutter, cut the dough the long way into ½-inch-thick (12 mm) pieces. Stretch and twist each piece to form thin breadsticks with a twirl of sesame seeds.
8. Bake the grissini on the prepared baking sheet for 15 minutes, or until golden brown, checking at the 10-minute mark to adjust the baking time if needed.

TIP

You can substitute the bread flour with all-purpose flour.

WHIPPED-FETA DIP TRIO

TOTAL TIME: 5 MINUTES **YIELD:** 3 BOWLS OF APPROXIMATELY 3 OUNCES (85 G) EACH

I am a huge whipped feta-dip fan! Its salty creaminess pairs beautifully with an endless combination of flavors, and lends itself to all types of crackers, breads, veggies, and more. It's also ridiculously easy to make using a food processor, taking under a few minutes to whip up something truly delicious.

½ cup (75 g) block feta cheese in brine
½ cup (115 g) cream cheese, at room temperature
1 tablespoon olive oil
1 tablespoon honey, warmed
1 tablespoon balsamic reduction
1 teaspoon dill

1. In a food processor, combine the feta, cream cheese, and olive oil until the cheeses are well combined and smooth.
2. Scoop 6 tablespoons (90 ml) of cheese out of the food processor onto each of 3 small plates or shallow bowls. Use a spoon to create a small well in the center of each.
3. Fill one well with honey, one with balsamic reduction, and the last one with dill.
4. Serve immediately with any bread or cracker of choice.

TIP

This dip pairs nicely with the Grissini Breadsticks recipe on page 101.

RECIPE

CHIMICHURRI SAUCE

TOTAL TIME: 10 MINUTES **YIELD:** ½ CUP (120 ML)

I'm just going to come right out and admit that I have a chimichurri addiction. Chimichurri is an Argentinian sauce similar to pesto but made with fresh parsley and cilantro instead of basil. This versatile salsa verde can elevate anything from pasta to meat, noodles to veggies. Let's make a big batch of this green magic.

- 1 cup (50 g) fresh Italian flat-leaf parsley leaves
- ¼ cup (10 g) fresh cilantro leaves
- 3 cloves garlic
- ½ medium red onion, roughly chopped
- 3 tablespoons fresh lemon juice
- ½ cup (120 ml) extra-virgin olive oil
- 1 teaspoon coarse sea salt or kosher salt
- ½ teaspoon red pepper flakes
- ¼ cup (60 ml) apple cider vinegar

1. In a food processor, chop the parsley, cilantro, garlic, and onion by pulsing and scraping down the sides as needed until finely chopped.
2. Add the lemon juice, olive oil, salt, red pepper flakes, and vinegar and pulse for 1 to 2 seconds or 2 to 3 times. This will keep the herbs bright, green, and finely chopped (rather than pulverized). Be careful not to overmix or you'll make more of a frothy oil.
3. Serve immediately or leave on the counter for a couple hours for the flavors to blend, then store in an airtight container for up to 10 days.

TIPS

You can substitute apple cider vinegar with red wine vinegar or white wine vinegar. For a traditional, handmade touch, use a mortar and pestle to grind the herbs while finely dicing the other ingredients. This sauce pairs wonderfully with the Chickpea Pasta Salad recipe on page 106 and the Smoked Pineapple Pork Skewers on page 105.

RECIPE

SMOKED PINEAPPLE PORK SKEWERS

TOTAL TIME: 1 HOUR AND 30 MINUTES **YIELD:** 8 TO 12 SKEWERS

There is a magic that happens when a sweet pineapple hits a grill paired with tender BBQ pork pieces and tangy red onions (and yes, drizzled with the Chimichurri Sauce from page 103). This is a combination of deliciousness that I just can't say no to. For this recipe, I used a smoker to cook the skewers, but you can absolutely use a traditional grill or oven to make it using the same temperatures.

1 pound (454 g) boneless pork chops, cut into 1-inch (2.5 cm) chunks
½ cup (120 ml) BBQ sauce of choice
1 large red onion, cut into 1-inch (2.5 cm) chunks
½ pineapple, cut into 1-inch (2.5 cm) chunks

1. In a large bowl, marinate the pork for 1 to 2 hours in the BBQ sauce.
2. Preheat the smoker, grill, or oven to 400°F (205°C).
3. Thread the pork chunks onto the skewers (see Note), alternating with chunks of red onion and pineapple in groups of three.
4. If using a grill or smoker, cook the pork skewers (with the grill lid closed) for 10 to 15 minutes, until cooked through, turning once. If cooking in the oven, place the skewers on a rimmed baking sheet and bake for 15 minutes. The internal temperature of the pork should be 165°F (74°C).
5. If using a smoker or grill and you'd like more caramelization, transfer the cooked skewers onto a baking sheet. Set the oven to broil on high heat and broil for 2 to 3 minutes, keeping a close watch to achieve your desired level of caramelization without burning. Serve immediately. If using an oven, follow the same broiling process after baking to add caramelization, then serve.

NOTE

If using a traditional grill, metal skewers are recommended, as they will not catch fire.

CHICKPEA PASTA SALAD

TOTAL TIME: 25 MINUTES **YIELD:** 6 TO 8 SERVINGS

This delicious and filling chickpea pasta salad is light, fresh, and filled with so many great summer staple veggies like crisp cucumber, sweet tomatoes, and tangy red onion. It is served at room temperature, making it another perfect al fresco dining recipe.

1 to 2 tablespoons salt
1 pack (12 ounces, or 28 g) uncooked rotini pasta
1 (15 ounces, or 425 g) can chickpeas, drained and rinsed
1 cup (145 g) diced red bell pepper
1 pint (270 g) grape tomatoes, cut in half
1 cup (150 g) diced cucumber
¼ cup (35 g) diced red onion
¼ cup (13 g) chopped fresh parsley
1 to 1½ cups (240 ml to 360 ml) Chimichurri Sauce (see page 103), to taste
Fresh herbs or nasturtium flowers, for garnish (optional)

1. Bring a large pot of salted water to a boil over medium-high heat, then cook the pasta according to the package instructions. Drain and rinse under cold water.
2. In a large bowl, add the chickpeas, pepper, tomatoes, cucumber, onion, and parsley. Add the cooled pasta to the bowl and toss until combined.
3. Add the chimichurri sauce and toss until everything is well coated.
4. Garnish with fresh herbs or nasturtium flowers, if desired. Serve and enjoy!

TIPS

To add some color, you can substitute the rotini with tricolor rotini. The red bell pepper can be replaced with any sweet or spicy pepper you love. This pasta salad is best served fresh but can be made a day ahead and stored in an airtight container in the fridge with little difference.

ROSEMARY LEMONADE FIZZ

TOTAL TIME: OVERNIGHT **YIELD:** 4 COCKTAILS

If you have never experienced the comingling flavors of rosemary and lemonade, prepare to fall in love, because rosemary-infused lemonade is a delight even on its own served over ice.

9 to 10 rosemary sprigs
2 cups (480 ml) lemonade of choice
Ice cubes
8 tablespoons (120 ml) gin or vodka
1 cup (240 ml) sparkling water
8 slices lemon, for garnish

1. Add 5 to 6 sprigs of rosemary to the lemonade and let infuse overnight in the fridge.
2. The following day, in each of the 4 glasses over ice, add 2 tablespoons of gin or vodka, ¼ cup (60 ml) of the rosemary-infused lemonade, and top with ¼ cup (60 ml) sparkling water. Stir well.
3. Add a sprig of rosemary to each.
4. Add a slice of lemon to each glass and a slice of lemon for the rim.

TIP

If you're using a taller glass, add more lemonade to fill it (about 1/2 cup, or 120 ml).

SUMMER BBQ

Eating outdoors is wonderful, especially when those pesky insects are cooperating. However, when they're not, and the rain is falling, or the wasps and mosquitos are swarming, it's also wonderful to host a BBQ dinner indoors. This way, you can incorporate a fun, seasonal theme, such as this floral-meets-citrus scene, into a sunny kitchen, screened-in porch, gazebo, or, like we do at home, set it up in the greenhouse!

Imagine the delight of your guests as they enjoy a vibrant meal surrounded by lush greenery, cheerful flowers, and the comforting ambiance of a cozy indoor space. An indoor setting for a summer BBQ can also provide a unique and charming atmosphere, making your gathering truly unforgettable.

BBQ CITRUS BASH

Summer BBQs, adorned with playful decor, foster a welcoming atmosphere of warmth and togetherness. As the evening sun stretches its glow into the extra hours, it sets the stage for creating lasting memories with friends and family. To capture the perfect bright summer vibe, consider transforming your dining space into a vibrant oasis with a citrus-themed tablescape. Let's dive into the details of crafting a stunning setup for your next BBQ gathering.

Florals

Summer is the perfect season for using all kinds of flowers, as this is the time that most flowers bloom. Get creative by using various colors and types of flowers for your arrangements. Some beautiful summer flowers that add some fun to your decor include:

* **Zinnias:** Heat-tolerant with a long vase life, available in a wide range of summer colors like yellow, pink, green, and purple
* **Sunflowers:** Stunning in sunny or white tones, perfect for summer arrangements
* **Queen Anne's lace:** Frilly white umbels add a whimsical touch, easily foraged or grown
* **Daisies and rudbeckia:** Bright whites to sunny yellows, embodying the essence of summer

These summer blooms will bring warmth, charm, and a burst of seasonal joy to your living space. Don't be afraid to mix textures, play with height, and go bold with your arrangements. Use the summer as a canvas for your BBQ masterpiece.

Colors, Centerpieces, and Decor Suggestions

The colors for your tablescape should reflect the liveliness that is this time of the year. Specific vibrant colors that work great are:

* Sunshine yellow
* Bright orange
* Lime green
* Cherry red
* Aqua blue
* Bright pink

You can easily incorporate these colors while also getting creative with the decor for this by using fruits to decorate your table. Fruits, such as oranges, limes, lemons, and grapefruit give the summer-inspired tablescape a unique touch while adding to the playfulness of this season.

You can place the fruits, either whole or sliced in half, over faux eucalyptus vines, which I've been using in my seasonal decor for many years, for visual interest. Citrus offers a beautiful spread that is also edible, compostable, economical, and sustainable. You can also use faux fruits, being mindful that you won't be able to cut them in half.

There's so much you can do with fruits this season to add some wonderful touches of color or decor and create a beautiful floral arrangement for your centerpiece. These fruits also fill the space with a delightful citrus aroma.

Summer-Kissed Floral Arrangement

Follow this quick guide to craft a stunning centerpiece that radiates charm and freshness.

1. Prepare the citrus stems: Cut limes and lemons in half through the middles. Insert wooden skewers into the bottoms of the halved fruits to serve as stems.
2. Arrange the citrus pieces in the center of your floral bouquet. These vibrant fruits will act as the focal points of your overall look.
3. Surround the citrus with delicate Queen Anne's lace to create texture and a soft, airy feel.
4. Add sunny, colorful zinnias to the arrangement for a pop of brightness and a cheerful touch.
5. Adjust the placement of all elements to ensure balance and harmony.

Tablecloth

To really make your scene stand out, you want to pick a tablecloth that helps you pop out the vibrant summer colors on your table. A pinstriped tablecloth lays a neutral base for my citrus-themed centerpiece and allows the fruits to take center stage. Here are more of my recommendations for tablecloths to use:

* **Solid tablecloth:** A white, tan, or neutral linen, soft green, soft orange, or light-yellow solid option, would all work well with the sunny citrus theme.
* **Patterned tablecloth:** A citrus-colored pinstripe or a dainty citrus pattern (like little lemons or oranges on a solid background) along with a citrus or black-and-white dotted pattern would be a great fit in this theme.

With the right tablecloth, your summer tablescape can go from simple to stunning. Whether you choose a solid hue or a playful pattern, let it complement the vibrant elements on your table and add the perfect touch.

Place Settings

Place settings are essential for setting the tone at a summer BBQ, adding both style and cohesion to your table while ensuring guests feel warmly welcomed.

For my setup, I started with green place mats as the foundation and layered them with round wicker chargers to introduce natural texture. I then added my everyday gray dinner and side plates, topped with a white saucer featuring a green rim for a coordinated look. To tie it all together, I included black-and-white pinstriped napkins, casually threaded through vintage citrus napkin rings. Finally, I tucked in faux-orange picks for a playful, vibrant finishing touch.

Here's my quick guide to re-create this look:

* Use natural materials like wicker or jute, either on their own or layered with a coordinating tone.
* Select a napkin that complements your neutral tone or secondary color, pairing it with a cute napkin ring or jute tie. Add a decorative element, such as a citrus pick or a sunny yellow flower, for extra charm.
* Stick to simple dishware in white, gray, or cream for versatility.
* Opt for casual yet elegant options like wineglasses and water glasses.
* Choose casual silverware, with silver or copper finishes working best to complement the overall theme.

These details ensure that your table radiates the summer vibes while also elevating your tablescape.

CITRUS FLORAL ICE-MOLD BOTTLE CHILLER

If you want to go even further with your citrus and floral theme for the summer BBQ, this addition to your beverage station only takes a few minutes to create, but will have all your guests oohing and ahhing over its beauty!

- 10 to 12 fresh or faux flowers of choice, blooms only, no stems required
- 5 to 10 mint sprigs or other herbs of choice
- 8 to 10 citrus slices
- Ice bottle mold
- 4½ cups (1 liter) boiled, reverse-osmosis filtered water, or distilled water (see Note)

1. Insert the flowers (I used calendula blossoms; see page 15), herbs, and citrus slices around the perimeter of the ice mold, pressing the blossoms and slices to the outside edge and adding the mint sprigs all around. The key to keeping everything in place is to add quite a lot of filler into the mold, so load up!
2. Transfer the mold to the freezer.
3. Bring the pitcher of 4½ cups of water to the freezer and fill the mold slowly with water. Allow to freeze overnight.
4. When you're ready to use it, place the ice mold into a bowl of warm water to release the ice.

NOTE

If you use distilled or reverse-osmosis water or boil your water and allow to cool first, your ice will be much clearer than with simple tap water, which can be quite cloudy once frozen.

CHEESY ONION BEER BREAD

TOTAL TIME: 1 HOUR AND 10 MINUTES **YIELD:** 1 LOAF, APPROXIMATELY 8 TO 10 SLICES

We are going to take homemade bread to new heights of simplicity and speed with this one bowl, no-yeast, no-knead, no-rise time, hearty loaf that's packed with flavor. This loaf goes way beyond your average dinner roll with its taste and texture, and really acts more like a side dish, perfect for mopping up sauces.

- 2½ cups (300 g) all-purpose flour
- 2 tablespoons granulated sugar
- 1 tablespoon baking powder
- 1 teaspoon salt
- 1½ cups (360 ml) beer of choice (a stronger beer will impart a stronger flavor)
- 2 tablespoons honey
- 1 cup (120 g) grated sharp cheddar cheese
- ½ cup (65 g) diced small onion
- 6 tablespoons unsalted butter, melted, divided

1. Preheat the smoker grill or oven to 350°F (175°C) and spray a 9 × 5-inch (23 × 12 cm) loaf pan with nonstick cooking spray.
2. In a medium mixing bowl, whisk the flour, sugar, baking powder, and salt until well combined and fluffed.
3. Stir in the beer and honey until the batter is just mixed. Be careful not to overmix. Gently stir in the cheese and onion.
4. Add half of the butter to the loaf pan and spoon in all the batter. Pour the remainder of the butter over the top of the batter.
5. Place the pan on the smoker grill or in the oven. Bake for 40 to 55 minutes, until the bread is golden brown and a toothpick inserted in the center comes out clean.
6. Let it cool slightly, for 5 to 8 minutes, before removing from the pan or serving.

TIP

If you've made the loaf ahead, I recommend heating it up in an oven set to 200°F (90°C) for 10 to 15 minutes before serving, to serve warm.

RECIPE

CHIPOTLE ORANGE–GLAZED SMOKED CHICKEN THIGHS

TOTAL TIME: 55 MINUTES **YIELD:** 4 TO 6 SERVINGS

Keeping with the citrus theme, I have here a failproof main dish that merges tangy orange flavor with spicy chipotle for the most incredibly tender chicken thigh recipe that will have everyone begging you for seconds.

8 boneless skinless chicken thighs
1½ teaspoons olive oil
2½ teaspoons poultry rub of choice
3 teaspoons salted butter
2 teaspoons orange marmalade
2 teaspoons canned chipotle in adobo sauce
¼ teaspoon salt
¼ teaspoon black pepper
2 tablespoons apple cider vinegar

1. Trim off any excess skin from the chicken thighs. Rub the thighs with the olive oil and season evenly with the poultry rub. Allow to marinate in a large bowl for 30 minutes.
2. In a small saucepan, combine the butter, marmalade, chipotle sauce, salt, pepper, and vinegar and cook on low heat for 3 to 4 minutes. Cover and turn off heat.
3. Preheat a pellet smoker to 275°F (135°C).
4. Place the chicken thighs directly on the smoker grill and cook for about 1½ hours, until the internal temperature reaches 150°F (66°C).
5. When the thighs are ready, transfer them to a cast-iron skillet filled with the glaze mixture. Using a brush, gently glaze the outside of the chicken thighs, remove from the skillet, and put them back into the smoker. Cook until the chicken temperature reaches 165°F (74°C).
6. Place the chicken back into the skillet and gently brush with the glaze. Then place the skillet into the oven set to broil on high heat for 2 to 3 minutes, watching carefully, to caramelize the glaze.
7. Serve immediately.

TIP

If you prefer, you can make this recipe in the oven. Cook the chicken at 350°F (175°C) in a skillet, following the same steps.

LEMON-HERB HASSELBACK POTATOES

TOTAL TIME: 1 HOUR TO 1 HOUR AND 45 MINUTES (DEPENDING ON POTATO SIZE AND OVEN)
YIELD: 8 SERVINGS

Hasselback potatoes, a delight with a fun backstory, originated at Stockholm's Hasselbacken restaurant in the 1950s. The story goes that a chef invented the idea of slicing a potato partway, fanning it out, and baking it. Since then, this technique spread across the world of potato lovers and we have been enjoying potatoes that are crispy on the outside and soft and tender on the inside. For this recipe, we're pairing them with lemon-garlic butter, adding a citrus flair and buttery goodness.

- 8 small to medium russet potatoes
- 3 to 4 tablespoons (45 to 60 ml) olive oil, divided
- 1 teaspoon sea salt, divided, plus more to taste
- ½ cup (1 stick, or 115 g) salted butter
- 4 cloves garlic, crushed
- 2 tablespoons fresh lemon juice, plus more to taste
- 2 tablespoons minced fresh parsley, divided
- 8 lemon wedges, for garnish

1. Preheat the oven to 400°F (205°C) and line a baking sheet with parchment paper.
2. Place a metal straw, chopstick, or pencil on either side of a potato; this will create a buffer, stopping the knife about ¼ inch (6 mm) above the cutting board, preventing you from cutting the potato all the way through. Using a sharp knife, make thin slices across the whole potato until you hit the buffer.
3. Place the potatoes on the baking sheet, then brush them with 1 ½ to 2 tablespoons of olive oil. Fan the potatoes out slightly and gently with your fingers to allow the olive oil to penetrate the slices. Sprinkle with ¼ teaspoon sea salt and slide them into the oven.
4. In a small saucepan, add the butter, garlic, lemon juice, and ¼ teaspoon sea salt, then cook on low heat until the butter has melted and everything is well combined. Turn off the heat and stir in half of the parsley.
5. Baste the potatoes with the remaining olive oil and sprinkle with ¼ teaspoon salt at the 15-minute and 30-minute marks as they bake.
6. After 30 minutes, switch to basting with the lemon-garlic butter every 15 minutes for another 30 to 60 minutes, depending on potato size and oven, or until the potatoes are tender when pierced with a knife. The slices will have separated during baking, allowing the lemon-garlic butter to penetrate deeply. Once the potatoes are tender, give them a final slathering with lemon-garlic butter and sprinkle with salt, to taste.
7. Serve with the remaining fresh parsley and lemon wedges.

TIP

For the sea salt, I recommend using Maldon Sea Salt Flakes.

NASTURTIUM VINAIGRETTE

TOTAL TIME: 10 MINUTES PLUS 1 TO 3 WEEKS FOR INFUSING **YIELD:** 1 PINT (568 ML)

As listed in my Must-Grow Edible Flowers list (page 15), nasturtiums are fully edible from the blossoms to the leaves and stems. They can be eaten fresh in salads, turned into pesto, or simply admired in the garden as vibrant, old-fashioned flowers. One way to use the peppery blossoms is in nasturtium flower–infused vinegar, which, when made with red and orange nasturtium blooms, becomes a striking and delicious color!

- 30 to 50 nasturtium blossoms, from your garden or from your local farmer's market (make sure they're organic)
- ¾ cup to 1 cup (180 ml to 240 ml) high-quality white vinegar

1. Place the nasturtium blossoms in a pint jar then cover with vinegar.
2. Cover the jar and let the flowers infuse for 1 to 3 weeks in a cool, dark place.
3. When you are ready to use the vinegar, strain out the flowers and store the infused vinegar in the same pint jar or an oil or vinegar bottle, which will make it easy to pour. It will last indefinitely!
4. Use to make salad dressings or marinades, or to splash on roasted veggies.

TIPS

Tap water can be quite cloudy once frozen, so for clearer ice, I recommend using distilled or reverse-osmosis water or boiled and cooled water. Also, for the white wine, I recommend using pinot grigio or sauvignon blanc.

FRESH-SQUEEZED CITRUS SANGRIA

TOTAL TIME: 2 HOURS AND 20 MINUTES **YIELD:** 6 SERVINGS

Sangria is the quintessential wine-based summer beverage, fresh, light, and pretty poured over fresh fruits. For this sangria, I've decided to take the presentation to a whole new level by creating citrus roses frozen in ice to act as the fruit addition in the glasses.

- 1 large ruby red grapefruit, for the rosette ice cubes
- 1 bottle (750 ml) white wine of choice
- ½ cup (120 ml) vodka
- ¾ cup (180 ml) sparkling water
- Juice from 3 freshly squeezed medium to large oranges, pulp strained
- Juice from 2 freshly squeezed medium to large ruby red grapefruits, pulp strained
- Juice from 1 freshly squeezed medium lime, pulp strained

1. To make the rosette ice cubes: Slice the grapefruit into thin rounds, starting at the blossom end, then halve the rounds. Arrange the larger half circles cut sides down around the outer edge of a muffin cup, overlapping them and moving inward with smaller half circles until you reach the center. Repeat as needed to create the desired number of roses.
2. Freeze the muffin tin for 10 minutes to set the roses.
3. Gently fill each cavity with water about two-thirds full. Freeze until fully set, about 2 hours.
4. To make the sangria: In a large pitcher, add the white wine, vodka, sparkling water, orange, grapefruit, and lime juices and stir.
5. Keep chilled and serve over the rosette ice cubes. If you made the bottle chiller craft on page 113, you can use it to keep the bottle perfectly chilled for serving.

FANTASTIC

BONFIRE NIGHT

One of the things I look forward to as the summer ends is sitting by the warmth and light of a bonfire on a cool late-summer evening: that short time in the season when it's warm enough to sit out for hours enjoying the firelight but also cool enough to snuggle up under a blanket on an Adirondack chair, as daydreams of the fall coziness ahead creep into your mind.

I cannot deny that once that fire is lit, it's hard not to immediately start craving all the classic bonfire staples. I'm talking smokies, sweet treats to roast on the fire, and of course, a warm drink that screams fall. And if we are going to celebrate the ending of a season, we might as well do it together with friends and family, commemorating it with fun and food done right!

So, without further ado. . .

CLASSIC UPSCALE HOT DOG BAR

Hot dogs are simple, but this high end–looking spread ups the esthetic ante on the average hot dog offering and takes assembling your dinner to a whole new world of hosting fun. So, while it's oh-so-easy, it's also oh-so-elevated.

To give your hot dog bar the upscale look your guests will love, there are a few key things to keep in mind and bring to the table; but remember, there is no way to go wrong with the setup and offerings on your hot dog bar. There are so many ways to get creative, so definitely have fun with it!

Setting the Mood for a Chic Hot Dog Bar

To elevate the casual nature of the food and spread and bring some glamour and style:

* Style your table with black and white serveware, adding black boards and cake stands and wire or wicker baskets to hold hot dogs and buns.
* Place all the condiments and hot dog toppings in a variety of white bowls and plates.
* Line baskets and stands with fun printed parchment/sandwich paper; I used a black and white backyard BBQ print. Find these easily online or in local dollar stores.
* Add candles in black tea-light holders or black cups for a soft glow.

With these simple elements, you can create a mood that brings hot dogs to a whole new level.

Ingredients to Make Your Hot Dog Bar a Successful Spread

This is a list of all the essential toppings that you can add to create a wonderful hot dog bar. Get creative with fun toppings and add any additional ones that you like to personalize it for your event or style.

Buns and wieners

* Variety of bakery hot dog buns (such as brioche, sesame, and Italian)
* Variety of hot dogs (such as chicken, pork, and beef)

Toppings

* Bacon, fried
* Red onions, fried
* Baked beans
* Pickles
* Shredded cheese
* Olives
* Ketchup
* Relish
* Yellow or Dijon mustard
* Hot sauce or other sauces of choice
* Chimichurri sauce
* Sides (such as chips, pasta salad, or mac and cheese)
* Onion dip or others of choice

Additional Toppings and Side Ideas (Not Shown)

* Jalapeños, hot banana peppers, or other peppers/pickled peppers
* Corn chips
* Queso
* Salsa
* Guacamole
* Popcorn
* Raw onions, diced
* Pickled onions

Prepping Directions

To prepare your hot dog bar, start by arranging the table and setting out all the sides and condiments that don't require cooking. Organize these items neatly on the table to ensure everything is accessible. Next, place your baskets and serveware so they're ready for the hot items to be added later. Once everything is visually arranged and ready to go, you're all set to bring in the freshly cooked hot dogs and start the fun!

Cooking Directions

To bring this yummy spread together, from sizzling bacon to caramelized onions, these steps ensure everything is cooked to delicious perfection. Follow the directions below to prep each element.

1. To cook the hot dogs: Grill the hot dogs on a BBQ or cook them in a skillet until they reach an internal temperature of 165°F (74°C). Place the cooked hot dogs in the oven to keep them warm.
2. To cook the bacon: In a large pan over medium heat, cook the bacon until lightly browned on one side. Flip and continue cooking until it reaches your desired crispness. Transfer the bacon to a baking tray and keep it warm in an oven set to 200°F (90°C). Place the bacon in the oven with the hot dogs to keep warm.
3. To cook the red onions: Thinly slice red onions (as many as needed) and sauté them in a skillet with a bit of oil over medium heat. Stir occasionally until they're soft and lightly caramelized, 10 to 12 minutes.
4. To heat the baked beans: In a small pot, heat the baked beans over medium heat, stirring frequently, until they are steaming.
5. Add the hot dogs, bacon, red onions, and baked beans to the hot dog bar in their allocated positions once you are ready to serve immediately.

Other Fun Things to Consider

To enhance your hot dogs and ensure your beautiful layout makes sense for serving, keep these tips in mind:

* Use paper plates and napkins in a fun coordinating theme, like black, white, or red, or red gingham for a bonfire BBQ vibe.
* Group condiments together and toppings together for serving ease.
* Add spoons and tongs on the side for serving.
* Have additional toppings and sides at the ready to refill or replace bowls as people serve themselves

HOMEMADE MARSHMALLOWS

TOTAL TIME: OVERNIGHT **YIELD:** ABOUT SIXTY 1-INCH (2.5 CM) SQUARES OR THIRTY 2-INCH (5 CM) SQUARES

Homemade marshmallows are the perfect way go all out during bonfire season. They're easy to make and customizable with any flavor extract. Essential tools you'll need are a stand mixer and a candy thermometer. The result? You will have marshmallows that are beautiful, simple, delectable, and giftable.

1 cup (120 g) confectioners' sugar, divided
⅓ cup (45 g) cornstarch
½ cup (120 ml) cold water
2½ tablespoons unflavored gelatin
⅔ cup (165 ml) light corn syrup
2 cups (400 g) granulated sugar
¼ teaspoon salt
2 teaspoons vanilla extract or extract of choice

1. Line a 9 × 13-inch (23 × 33 cm) pan with oversized parchment paper so it's hanging over the ends of the pan. (This will help you later to pull the marshmallows out.) Spray it liberally with nonstick cooking spray, making sure not to miss any spots.
2. In a small bowl, whisk together ½ cup (100 g) of the confectioners' sugar and the cornstarch. Set aside. In the bowl of a stand mixer fitted with a whisk attachment, pour the ½ cup (120 ml) cold water, then add the gelatin. Let it bloom until firm, 8 to 10 minutes.
3. In a medium saucepan, mix ½ cup (120 g) of water and the corn syrup. Pour the granulated sugar into the center of the saucepan and add the salt. Bring the mixture in the saucepan to a boil over medium-high heat and boil until the sugar has dissolved completely and the syrup reaches 240°F (116°C), 8 to 10 minutes. Do not stir the mixture.
4. Set the stand mixer to low speed and carefully pour the hot syrup directly onto the bloomed gelatin, trying to keep it from the sides of the bowl as much as possible. Slowly increase the speed to high and continue to whip the mixture until it is thick, white, and glossy, 10 to 12 minutes, scraping down the bowl as needed. Add the vanilla or extract of choice and mix until just incorporated, 1 minute.
5. Quickly scrape the mixture into your prepared pan using a silicone spatula that has been sprayed with nonstick cooking spray. It is essential to work quickly, as the marshmallow will begin to set up and become difficult to transfer. Smooth the top into an even layer immediately. Sift half of the confectioners' sugar and cornstarch mix evenly across the marshmallow slab to coat. Cover the pan loosely with plastic wrap and let sit overnight at room temperature.

TIPS

Marshmallows can be stored at room temperature in an airtight container or zip-top bag for up to 2 weeks. If you plan to roast them or put them in hot cocoa, you can allow them to dry open at room temperature for 1 to 2 days longer. They will stand up to heat better when they are drier. They are also giftable if you put them into clear cookie bags and tie them with a piece of fabric or string!

6. The following day, line a cutting board with parchment paper and turn the marshmallow slab onto it, peeling off the top parchment. Sift the remaining confectioners' sugar and cornstarch mix over the marshmallow slab, coating well.
7. Using a pizza cutter, dough scraper, or a sharp knife sprayed with nonstick cooking spray, cut into 1-inch (2.5 cm) or 2-inch (5 cm) strips one way, and then across the other way for square marshmallows.
8. Place the remaining ½ cup confectioners' sugar in a large zip-top bag. Working with 3 or 4 marshmallows at a time, toss the marshmallows in the bag with the confectioners' sugar, then toss in a fine-mesh strainer to remove any excess powder.

RECIPE

CRISPY RICE TREATS S'MORES SPHERES

TOTAL TIME: 20 MINUTES **YIELD:** 24 BALLS

The moment I confirmed that you could roast rice crispy squares on the fire, I knew that they needed to be made round and filled with a chocolate center to complete the s'more transformation. You heard it here first! These are the perfect marshmallow treats to pop on a skewer or stick and hover over a flame, but even just as is, they are a delicious and fun surprise to bite into for any chocolate lover.

- ¼ cup (½ stick, 55 g) unsalted butter, plus more for coating
- 1 package (12 ounces, or 340 g) marshmallows
- 1 teaspoon vanilla extract
- 6 cups (180 g) crispy rice cereal (such as Rice Krispies)
- 2 to 3 squares (57 to 85 g) semisweet baking chocolate bars (such as Baker's)
- 1 tablespoon cooking oil of choice, to grease your hands

1. In a large saucepan, melt the butter over low heat. Add all the marshmallows and stir frequently until completely melted and well blended. Remove the pan from the heat, stir in the vanilla, and then add the cereal, mixing until the cereal is fully coated.
2. Using a lightly buttered spatula, spread the mixture loosely onto a sheet of parchment paper placed on a countertop or other hard surface.
3. Chop the chocolate into ¼-inch (6 mm) cubes and set aside.
4. Pour the cooking oil into a bowl and lightly grease your hands. Once the rice crispy mixture has cooled slightly (about 5 minutes) and is sticking together, quickly grab a golf ball–size portion of the mixture. Place a chocolate cube in the center, then fold the mixture around it and roll it into a ball. Place each ball onto a separate sheet of parchment paper to cool completely (about 10 minutes).
5. Serve as is, or enjoy next to a bonfire or wood-burning fireplace for a cozy treat.

RECIPE

FIRESIDE S'MOREGASBORD

TOTAL TIME: 10 MINUTES **YIELD:** 6 TO 8 SERVINGS

Here, we are taking the basic s'mores offerings of graham crackers, chocolate, and marshmallows and kicking it up a notch by including a variety of roast-able additions to the spread. This is one of the easiest boards to set up, and with a little fireside table, it has everything anyone could want to snack on as they sit by the fire! Everyone will be wanting s'more s'mores!

- 1 bag (14 ounces, or 400 g) large marshmallows or 60 homemade marshmallows (see page 126)
- 24 Crispy Rice Treats S'mores Spheres (see page 129)
- ¾ cup (180 ml) fig jam (such as Bonne Maman)
- 12 snack-sized cheeses (such as Babybel) in your preferred flavors
- 2 boxes of 2 types (40 to 50) crackers of choice (such as pretzel crackers and club crackers)
- 1 box (20 to 24) honey graham wafers/crackers (such as Honey Maid)
- 12 chocolate-covered graham cookies (such as Celebration)
- 16 chocolate-covered and caramel- or cappuccino-filled cookies (such as Celebration)
- 2 cups (100 g) mini marshmallows

1. Place all the large marshmallows into a large bowl and position the bowl in the left corner of the board. Add the rice crispy balls to a smaller bowl and place it on the right side of the board.
2. Position a small bowl on a plate and fill it with fig jam. Surround the jam with the snack-sized cheeses.
3. Tuck one type of crackers and all the cookies into small bowls and arrange these bowls around the board. Use the remaining crackers and graham crackers to form arcs around the perimeter of the board.
4. Arrange a line of chocolate-covered graham cookies down the middle of the board and pour mini marshmallows into the board, filling any gaps.
5. Serve immediately and enjoy!

RECIPE

BOOZY HOT CHOCOLATE

TOTAL TIME: 5 MINUTES **YIELD:** 1 CUP (240 ML)

In my house, we love hot chocolate (and all frothy hot beverages!), so a few years ago, I bought a milk- and beverage-frothing machine. Little did I know that it would revolutionize the way my kids and I made our hot chocolates. So, even though you don't need a frothing machine to make this hot chocolate, I do highly recommend using one, because the froth really makes it better!

- ¾ cup (180 ml) 2% milk
- 2 tablespoons hot chocolate mix
- 2 tablespoons Irish cream (such as Baileys)
- 2 tablespoons rum-and-coffee liqueur (such as Kahlua)
- 10 mini marshmallows or homemade marshmallows (see page 126), for topping
- Whipped cream, for topping
- Caramel sauce, for topping
- Chocolate shavings, for topping

1. In a small pot, heat the milk over medium-low heat for 5 minutes, being careful not to bring to a boil. Turn the heat off when the temperature is how you like it, then mix in the hot chocolate powder, stirring well until fully combined.
2. In a mug, add the Irish cream and rum-and-coffee liqueur, then pour the hot chocolate over the mixture.
3. Place the mini marshmallows on a small baking sheet. Use a small kitchen torch or torch lighter to lightly roast them.
4. Top your hot chocolate with whipped cream, a drizzle of caramel sauce, chocolate shavings, and mini marshmallows.
5. Serve with a teaspoon and enjoy!

TIP

You can use a milk-frother to make the hot chocolate or use a hand-held frothing tool to whip it up.

FALL

Fall arrives full force in a blaze of colors. Burnt oranges, rust reds, deep yellows, and the richest earthy shades of green and brown come together in a symphony of warm tones. I adore this season, as it gives us time to reflect on a summer well lived and to look forward to the holidays. The season brings the full harvest and preparations for winter. Maybe this is why autumn flavors are so warm, spiced, fragrant, and full, getting us ready for the cold days ahead. If fall's signature style is cozy, its love language is comfort food.

HARVEST DINNER

An ideal way to ring in this cozy season is making a fall-themed harvest dinner. The menu boasts casual fare packed with maximum taste and irresistible freshness. It's a wonderful celebration of robust flavors and dishes made from the garden's best late-season offerings.

For a harvest dinner on a warm, early-autumn day, nothing compares to the beauty of eating under a canopy of changing leaves. Be sure to invite everyone to arrive with cozy sweaters in hand to enjoy the fresh fall air and put them on as needed.

A chorus of "mmmmmm" and "this is so good" is a fine way to say goodbye to summer and hello to autumn.

HARVEST GATHERING

When the air gets crisp and the leaves start to change, there's no better way to celebrate the season than with a beautifully set fall-themed table. In my home, this means lugging our big wooden patio table and deck chairs out under the colorful trees, creating a wondrous spot to sit down and truly soak in the fall in celebration. To help you create your own enchanting fall tablescape, follow these simple steps that will infuse your space with the cozy and inviting essence of the season.

Florals

Autumn offers beautiful florals in all the colors of the season, and the following recommendations are options that I most love to incorporate into my fall-themed tablescapes.

* **Echinacea:** This large, daisy-like flower comes in all the hues of fall, from warm, deep purples and burgundies to deep yellows and rust reds.
* **Chrysanthemum:** A top flower that comes to mind for fall is the chrysanthemum, in all its varieties, from dainty flowers to large, billowy blooms. With their abundant flowers in purply burgundies, oranges, whites, and warm yellows, they add a beautiful touch to fall arrangements and decor.
* **Sunflowers:** Late-summer and early-fall sunflowers come in varieties like Autumn Beauty and Velvet Queen and boast blooms that range from the deepest burgundies to rust reds and burnt oranges.
* **Foliage:** You can also recruit all types of fall foliage on trees and shrubs, snipping branches and stems to use in arrangements.

Colors

The essence of this bountiful season is captured through warmer colors. Some beautiful colors that add to the richness of this season include:

* Deep burgundies
* Olive, forest, and deep sage greens
* Mustard or warm deep yellows
* Rust reds
* Neutral browns
* Bright pumpkin and burnt oranges

Any of these colors work great to set the tone of your table decor and capture the palette of the fall season.

Centerpieces and Decor Suggestions

The ideal centerpiece for your fall-themed table should have a combination of cozy lighting and natural elements. You want the lighting to be spread throughout the table, creating an enchanting vibe, while natural elements surround it to complete the fall look. The following lighting choices work wonderfully:

* Large wooden pillar candles
* Tea lights
* Rustic candles
* Twinkle lights

Some additional natural fall elements to consider adding to your table:

* Pumpkins
* Apples
* Pears
* Acorns

For my table, I arranged my centerpiece by adding large wooden pillar candles down the center, surrounded by cute orange pumpkins, placed over a faux green vine garland. I wound a string of twinkle lights all around the centerpiece and added a couple of additional wooden tea lights for added glow.

Tablecloth

A fall-themed tablecloth works great to set the scene and guide your overall tablescape look. For my table, I used a black, orange, and green pumpkin-themed tablecloth. You can't go wrong with anything pumpkin during this time of year! You can also use other fall-themed tablecloths, such as a:

* **Solid tablecloth:** Fall-toned solid tablecloths in deep tones like burgundy, burnt orange, deep greens, dark browns, or tan will complement and accentuate rich warm florals and bright pumpkins.
* **Patterned tablecloth:** Look for fall leaf–motif tablecloths boasting various rich autumn colors, pumpkin print, gingham print in a deep fall color, or a fall-toned floral print.

Place Settings

Creating the perfect place settings is essential for tying your table's theme together and enhancing the overall ambiance of your gathering. For my setup, I leaned into earthy, rich tones to complement the woodsy vibe.

For the place settings, I layered rattan place mats over wood place mats to continue the natural theme. I used deep-green dinner plates under black side plates—all placed beside green pinstriped napkins to maintain the rich and deep color palette. Amber water glasses and amber wineglasses completed the look, ready for enjoying a delightful sip of wine under the trees.

To achieve this same type of look on your table, you can use:

* A burlap or neutral table runner
* Earthy, natural place mats like wood, burlap, or rattan, layered if you wish
* Deep-, dark-, or fall-toned plates, layered in different shades
* Patterned napkins in coordinating fall colors to match your theme
* Gold, black, or copper cutlery for striking contrast
* Glassware in smoked, amber, or fall hues—feel free to mix two tones for added interest

HOMEMADE BREAD BOWLS

TOTAL TIME: 2 HOURS AND 11 MINUTES **YIELD:** 8 BOWLS

These simple homemade bread bowls can easily be whipped up early in the day so they are ready to serve with dinner.

- 2½ cups (600 ml) warm water
- 2 teaspoons granulated sugar
- 1½ tablespoons active dry yeast
- 2 teaspoons salt
- 2 tablespoons olive oil, plus more for greasing the bowl
- 6 to 7 cups (810 to 945 g) bread flour, divided, plus more for shaping and kneading
- 1 large egg
- 1 tablespoon 2% milk

1. In the bowl of a stand mixer fitted with a dough hook, combine the water, sugar, and yeast. Stir well, then let sit for 5 to 10 minutes, until the yeast is foamy. Add the salt, oil, and 2 cups (270 g) of the bread flour. Stir on medium-low, scraping the sides with a spatula, until mixed well. Continue to add the remaining flour and mixing on low until a nice soft dough forms. You may not need all the flour; stop adding it when a smooth dough starts to form.
2. Knead on medium-low for 8 minutes. The dough should be kneading clean from the sides of the bowl. If it's too sticky, add a bit more flour until it's not. Grease a large bowl lightly with olive oil. Transfer the dough to the bowl and cover with plastic wrap. Let rise in a warm spot for 40 minutes until doubled in size.
3. Punch down the dough to remove air bubbles, and lay the dough out onto a lightly floured surface in a disk shape and divide into 8 equal wedges, like a pizza. Roll each section of dough into a ball and transfer to baking sheets lined with parchment paper, leaving 2 inches (5 cm) of space to allow for the dough to rise. Loosely cover with a flour sack or tea towel and let the dough rise for another 30 to 45 minutes, until doubled in size again.
4. Preheat the oven to 400°F (205°C) while the bread bowls are rising. In a small bowl, whisk the egg up well with the milk to create a wash; brush this onto the risen bread bowls just before putting them in the oven. Be sure to evenly coat the bread bowls as they will be shiny wherever the wash is applied, and even looks best! Bake for 22 to 26 minutes, until golden brown on top.
5. Cool for 15 minutes, then use a sharp serrated knife to cut lids off the top of each bowl. Remove some of the bread inside the bread to make space for soup.

TIPS

You can premake these bread bowls or freeze half the batch for use later by stopping after step 3 and placing the dough balls in a zip-top bag in the freezer. Thaw and complete the rest of the steps at a later time for fresh bread bowls in a flash! For the cutouts, I love to use a wide-mouth mason jar lid as a guide. You can also substitute the bread flour for 6 to 7 cups (720 to 840 g) of all-purpose flour.

TIP

You can serve this soup in Homemade Bread Bowls (see page 141).

RECIPE

HEARTY BUTTERNUT SQUASH SOUP

TOTAL TIME: 1 HOUR **YIELD:** 8 TO 10 CUPS (2 L TO 2.4 L)

This thick and creamy soup is my children's favorite, and it always brings me joy to see them eat such a healthy, high-fiber, protein-ful, and vegetable-packed meal! The key to the incredible amount of flavor in this soup is caramelizing the squash, onions, and garlic on the stove before pureeing. I also find that this method speeds up preparation compared to roasting the squash in the oven.

- 1 whole butternut squash, peeled, seeded, and cut into ¾-inch (2 cm) chunks
- ½ cup (1 stick, or 115 g) salted or unsalted butter, cut into ½-inch (12 mm) cubes, divided
- 1 medium white or yellow onion, diced
- 3 cloves garlic, crushed
- 1 box (32 ounces, or 960 ml) chicken broth, divided
- 1 teaspoon chili powder
- 1 teaspoon ground cumin
- 1 teaspoon curry powder
- 1 teaspoon salt, plus more to taste
- 1 cup (135 g) canned or frozen corn, drained
- 1 cup (170 g) canned black beans, rinsed and drained
- 1 cup (135 to 145 g) fresh or frozen peas
- Shredded cheddar cheese, for topping
- Chives, for topping

1. Heat a large stainless-steel pan over medium to medium-high heat for 2 to 3 minutes. Add the squash and ¼ cup (½ stick, or 55 g) of butter to the pan, stirring and moving the squash as soon as it starts to brown, 8 to 10 minutes. The goal is to lightly brown the squash without burning it. Once the squash chunks are browned on the sides, add the remaining ¼ cup (½ stick, or 55 g) butter, the onions, and garlic. Sauté until the onions become transparent and just start to brown, about 5 to 7 minutes.
2. Add half the box of chicken broth to the squash mixture, the chili powder, cumin, curry powder, and salt. Stir and simmer for 5 minutes.
3. Transfer the soup to a blender or use an immersion blender to completely puree the soup.
4. Return the soup to the pan and heat it over medium-low heat. Add the remaining chicken broth and stir well to combine.
5. Stir in the corn, beans, and peas. Mix well and then simmer for 10 to 15 minutes, occasionally stirring and scraping the sides back down into the soup until the soup begins to thicken to your liking.
6. Top with shredded cheddar and chives and serve.

HARVEST APPLE SALAD

TOTAL TIME: 10 TO 15 MINUTES **YIELD:** 4 TO 6 SERVINGS

This fresh salad is an ode to the season with a cacophony of harvest flavors, from the Gala apples to the toasted pine nuts. This whole salad is brought together by a creamy, tangy apple cider vinaigrette that is about to become your new favorite dressing!

FOR THE SALAD

8 to 10 cups (320 to 400 g) red and green lettuce blend
2 medium apples, thinly sliced (Gala or any tart, crisp variety)
1 cup (150 g) crumbled feta cheese
2 medium carrots, thinly sliced
½ cup (70 g) dried cranberries
⅓ cup (45 g) toasted pine nuts

FOR THE DRESSING

⅓ cup (75 ml) olive oil
3 tablespoons apple cider vinegar
2 tablespoons honey
2 tablespoons Greek yogurt
1 tablespoon mayonnaise
1 tablespoon Dijon mustard
½ teaspoon crushed garlic
Salt and black pepper, to taste

1. To make the salad: Wash and dry the lettuce, then place it in a large salad bowl.
2. Thinly slice the apples and place them in groups of 8 to 10 slices evenly around the lettuce. Sprinkle the feta in groupings alongside the apples.
3. Use a vegetable peeler to create long, wide slices from the carrots. Roll them up and place them around the salad.
4. Add the dried cranberries and toasted pine nuts.
5. To make the dressing: In a small bowl, whisk together the olive oil, apple cider vinegar, honey, Greek yogurt, mayonnaise, Dijon mustard, and garlic, adding salt and pepper to taste.
6. Liberally spoon dressing across the salad and serve.

RECIPE

CARROT CAKE DONUTS

TOTAL TIME: 45 MINUTES **YIELD:** 12 DONUTS

When I realized I could make any cake or muffin recipe in a donut pan I was so excited at the world of opportunity for presentation—and with the idea of using carrot cake, I was especially inspired! I added calendula petals as a garnish. These resilient flowers bloom late into fall, are adorable, and have anti-inflammatory benefits. The full flowers are removed before eating, but how pretty!

FOR THE DONUTS

½ cup (120 ml) avocado oil, plus more for greasing if needed
1 ¼ cups (150 g) all-purpose flour
½ teaspoon baking powder
½ teaspoon baking soda
½ teaspoon salt
1 teaspoon ground cinnamon, plus more for garnish (optional)
½ teaspoon ground clove
½ teaspoon ground nutmeg
¼ cup (55 g) packed light brown sugar
¾ cup (150 g) granulated sugar
2 large eggs, at room temperature
1 teaspoon vanilla extract
2 cups (220 g) finely shredded carrots
Calendula blossoms, for garnish (optional)
Crushed nuts of choice, for garnish (optional)

FOR THE FROSTING

½ cup (115 g) cream cheese, at room temperature
¼ cup (30 g) confectioners' sugar

1. To make the donuts: Preheat the oven to 350°F (175°C). Spray two 6-cavity donut tins with nonstick cooking spray or lightly coat with avocado oil.
2. In a medium bowl, stir together the flour, baking powder, baking soda, salt, cinnamon, cloves, and nutmeg until well combined.
3. In a large mixing bowl, combine the brown sugar, granulated sugar, avocado oil, eggs, and vanilla and mix.
4. Add the dry ingredients to the wet ingredients, mixing lightly. Fold in the shredded carrots and combine just until mixed. Be sure not to overmix to keep your batter light and spongey.
5. Transfer the batter into a piping bag or zip-top bag with a corner cut off, and pipe the batter in a circle within each donut cavity until they are ¾ full.
6. Bake for 12 to 15 minutes. Let cool in the pan for 5 minutes, then transfer to a wire rack to cool completely, about 15 minutes.
7. To make the frosting: In a shallow bowl, stir together the cream cheese and confectioners' sugar until you have a soft frosting.
8. Dip the donuts in the frosting to coat or use an offset spatula to spread it. Garnish with calendula blossoms or petals, cinnamon, or crushed nuts.

MUSHROOM MERINGUES

TOTAL TIME: 2 ½ TO 3 HOURS **YIELD:** 30 TO 35 MINI MUSHROOMS

Fall is a great time for fungi, but if you're not up to hunting, identifying, cleaning, and cocking real mushrooms, you can do the next best thing: Make mushroom lookalike cookies!

2 egg whites

½ cup (100 g) granulated sugar

⅛ teaspoon salt

⅛ teaspoon cream of tartar

2 squares semisweet chocolate, for melting and assembling the meringues

Cocoa, for sprinkling

1. Preheat the oven to 200°F (90°C). Line a baking sheet with parchment paper and set it aside for piping in Step 4.
2. In a mixer bowl with a whisk attachment, add the egg whites, sugar, salt, and cream of tartar. Whisk on high until the mixture becomes fluffy, white, and shiny, and peaks form when you lift some of the mixture with a spoon.
3. Add the batter to a piping bag with a large round tip, or a zip-top bag with a small corner cut off.
4. For the mushroom tops: Pipe 1- to 1 ½-inch (2.5 to 4 cm) rounds with low dome shapes, resembling mushroom caps, onto the parchment paper.
5. For the mushroom bottoms: Pipe bases approximately ¾ inch (2 cm) wide, shaped like taller Hershey's kisses. Ensure they are upright rather than leaning to help your mushrooms stand properly. You can vary the sizes, making some shorter and some taller, for a natural look.
6. Dip your finger in water and use it to smooth the tops of the mushroom caps, ensuring they are flat and free of peaks before baking.
7. Bake for 90 to 120 minutes, until they are hard to the touch and come off the parchment easily. Let them cool completely, about 30 minutes.
8. In a small, microwave-safe bowl, melt the chocolate in the microwave for 30 to 40 seconds, stirring and then microwaving for another 10 to 15 seconds if required.
9. Create a little hole in the bottom of each mushroom cap with a pointy knife, then fill the holes with the chocolate. Quickly press the bottoms into the holes to attach to the mushroom tops.
10. Sprinkle cocoa on the mushroom tops to make the mushrooms look authentic and serve!

TIP

You can replace granulated sugar with caster sugar.

HALLOWEEN

Hosting Halloween get-togethers is truly the most fang-tastic way to celebrate the spooky season. For many years, I have hosted a big Halloween party, going all out with an outdoor candy hunt, food, and fun. It's one event that my kids start asking about months in advance. Everyone, from the kids to the adults, dresses up and gets right into the spirit of this holiday.

My preferred Halloween esthetic is to create the feeling of stumbling into a witch's lair. I mix traditional, fright-filled elements like skeletons and black decor with natural, earthy witchcraft vibes, such as tarot cards, palmistry paraphernalia, unique greenery, and dried dead florals, all with a spooky touch. But it isn't just about the thrills and chills.

Halloween in our home is a chance to get dressed up, be a little weird, and bring big pumpkin smiles to the faces of all our friends and family who join us here for gatherings, big and small.

SPOOKY-FEST

Transport your guests to an ambiance that is both festive and frightful with a hauntingly beautiful Halloween-themed decor. Set the scene for an unforgettable night by mixing traditional Halloween elements with elegant touches. Here are my tips for creating a spooky yet sophisticated table.

Florals

Halloween is the perfect time to get a little spooky and wild with your flower arrangement choices. Below are some fun floral options to setting up a spook-tacular table.

* **Dried florals:** From hydrangeas in whites or greens to deep-purply strawflowers or statice to orange Chinese lanterns, dried flowers can lend a spooky pop of Halloween color to arrangements.
* **Branches:** Twisted branches lend to the ideal Halloween vibe.
* **Succulents and vines:** These plants are often available in eerie shapes and can be added to potted arrangements or draped from your vase.
* **Seed pods:** Queen Anne's lace, poppies, and other florals left to go to seed add a dark element.
* **Black roses:** This dark twist on the typical romantic flower adds the perfect dramatic touch to your Halloween table.
* **Dark red calla lilies or dahlias:** These flowers are the perfect mix of sophistication and mystery.

These botanical touches are sure to enchant your guests and add a spooky charm to your setup.

Colors

As you create your go-to Halloween table decor collection, I recommend picking decorative items for your collection in the following colors:

* Blacks
* Grays
* Whites

This way if you want to reuse the decor and add new items, everything continues to coordinate with the tones. Additional Halloween-themed tones are:

* Pumpkin orange
* Deep purple

These colors work wonderfully for creating a witchy-themed dinner table that is both fun and terror-rrific.

Centerpieces and Decor Suggestions

Along with Halloween-themed colors, you'll also want to make sure you're creating a scare-rrific atmosphere, in an elegant way, of course. Here are my quick tips for adding decor for this type of setup.

1. Set up your table outdoors to embrace the seasonal atmosphere. For my setup, I placed a table on our giant chessboard patio, surrounded by string lights and falling leaves, creating a magical and moody backdrop.

2. Down the center of the table, arrange a mix of black-and-white skull hurricane vases. If you don't want to do skulls, you can always choose another halloween-themed element to include down the center of your table arrangement, such as faux cobwebs and spiders or mini witch hats.
3. Add coordinating tall taper candle holders in shades of white ceramic, black, and gold, alongside white ceramic tea-light holders.
4. Add a festive flair by interspersing these elements with mini white pumpkins.
5. Craft a quirky centerpiece. Use a large black ceramic vase and fill it with a mix of elements like trailing succulents, fragrant herbs, seed pods, and "dead" or dried plants. This adds an eerie yet stylish touch to your centerpiece. Position the vase in the center for a balanced and dramatic setup.

Tablecloth

To complete your spooky-elegant vibes, lay all your decor on a Halloween-themed skull-print tablecloth in black and gray to tie the whole look together. Other tablecloths that you could use for this type of setup are:

* **Solid tablecloths:** This type of tablecloth in black, dark gray, deep green, or deep purple works great for a witchy or spooky theme. Linen is always a wonderful choice, but as a cooler season has set in, thicker fabrics like a brocade or twill work well too.
* **Patterned tablecloths:** For Halloween there are so many fun options for patterned tablecloths like ghost print, pumpkin print, skull print, skeleton print, bat print, and more. I recommend sticking to prints with mainly blacks, whites, and grays for easy use from year to year with different florals and accessories.

Once you've selected the ideal tablecloth to set the foundation for your Halloween theme, you can elevate the look with enchanting place settings.

Place Settings

Witchy place settings are a key element in creating an enchanting Halloween tablescape, bringing a sense of mystery and drama that sets the mood for the entire setup. Follow these quick tips to create an enchanting Halloween affair filled with witchy charm.

1. **Start with a base:** Use black cotton braided round place mats or opt for earthy textures like burlap, rattan, or wood for a natural touch.
2. **Layer your plates:** Choose plates in coordinating tones such as black, gray, or white, layering them for depth and dimension.
3. **Add napkins**: Incorporate napkins in black, white, gray, or a patterned design that matches your tablecloth. Fold them neatly and tie the look together with a spooky or elegant touch.
4. **Top with mini pumpkins:** Place a white or orange mini pumpkin on each plate stack for a festive and eye-catching detail.
5. **Incorporate vases and florals:** Use vases in black, gray, or glass and fill them with spooky, dramatic florals or dried arrangements to emphasize the theme.
6. **Enhance with candlelight:** Add a variety of candle holders—tapers, pillars, hurricanes, or tea lights—in black, gray, white, or gold to create a cozy and mysterious ambiance.
7. **Choose the right cutlery:** Opt for gold or black cutlery to add contrast and elegance to the place settings.
8. **Use statement glassware:** Include glassware in smoked, amber, or fall hues, mixing tones if desired for added visual interest.

TEA FOR BOO!
BOOTEAFUL!
BOOTEAFUL!

CRAFT

GIFTABLE TEA GHOSTS

These adorable little ghosts make a fantastic spooky gift for friends, coworkers, and teachers. They're also a great quick craft for kids to help with. This cool giftable makes three tea bags.

BOO-TEA-FUL GHOST BLEND INGREDIENTS

2½ teaspoons dried lemon balm leaves

2½ teaspoons black tea leaves

2½ teaspoons cinnamon chips

1½ teaspoons crushed dried apple

ITEMS

3 white coffee filters

Butcher's twine

Paint pens

Card stock

Pinking shears or scissors

Hole puncher

Mason jar

6- to 8-inch (15 to 20 cm) piece of patterned fabric of choice (optional)

1. To make the tea blend: In a medium bowl, mix the lemon balm, black tea, cinnamon chips, and crushed apple until well combined.
2. To make the ghosts: Add 2 tablespoons of the tea blend to the center of a white coffee filter. Fold the filter around the tea to create a ball at the top, and twist the filter underneath. Secure with butcher's twine.
3. To make the tea tags: Print Halloween-themed words (or use paint pens) on card stock, such as "Booteaful" and "Tea for Boo", and cut the card stock using pinking shears or scissors to make little tags. Use a hole puncher to make a hole on each tag and add twine to attach to the tea ghosts.
4. Place the ghosts standing upright in a mason jar and seal, using fabric to decorate the top, if desired.
5. To make the tea: Steep tea ghosts in a mug with boiling water, covered, for 2 to 4 minutes. Remove the tea ghost if you wish, or leave it for a stronger tea, and enjoy!

TIP

These giftable tea ghosts can be done with any tea blend!

RECIPE

SCARECUTERIE

TOTAL TIME: 15 MINUTES **YIELD:** 6 TO 8 SERVINGS

Here, a simple meat, cheese, and bread board gets a terrifying upgrade that makes it so fun to dig into. It's hard to believe how realistic these salami rosette eyeballs are and how easy they are to make!

4 mozzarella bocconcini cheese balls
4 green olives with pimentos
54 salami slices, to create the rosettes
1 whole-grain artisanal bakery baguette, sliced
1 white artisanal bakery baguette, sliced

1. Using a large metal smoothie straw or a knife, cut a hole in each cheese ball slightly smaller than the size of an olive so the olive squeezes into the hole to fit snugly inside. Press an olive into each hole in the cheese, making sure the pimento is facing upward.
2. Place the 4 eyeballs onto your board, platter, or cake stand.
3. To create the salami rosettes: Using a champagne flute, fold a piece of salami over the rim, and press it down on each side of the glass. Repeat this process, overlapping each piece of salami by 35 percent until you've gone around the glass twice; you'll need about 6 slices of salami to make each rosette. Invert the glass over an olive eyeball on your board and remove the glass. Repeat to make 3 more eyeball rosettes. Arrange them in a group in the center.
4. Make 4 more plain salami rosettes and arrange them to the top, left, and right of the eyeball rosettes.
5. Add a circle of sliced baguettes around the rosettes, alternating white and whole grain. Serve and enjoy!

TIPS

If I am entertaining a larger group, I like to make this main display alongside a side bowl of olive and cheese eyeballs using mini-bocconcini (so there is enough for everyone to enjoy). I'll add another plate of simply rolled salami. This helps your main display last a little longer if you are entertaining a crowd. I'll also sometimes add a few dips or condiments in bowls alongside this display for the breads.

MINI PUFF-PASTRY PIZZA PUMPKIN BITES

TOTAL TIME: 28 MINUTES **YIELD:** 9 TO 12 BITES

These cute little pizza pumpkins are such a hit for little and big fingers alike. It's a fun recipe to surprise the kids with a spooky-season after-school snack, along with being a great Halloween party appetizer!

1 sheet (12-inch, or 30.5 cm) puff pastry, thawed
2 tablespoons pizza sauce
12 small pepperoni slices
¼ cup (30 g) light mozzarella cheese, finely grated
Stems from 9 to 12 cherry, mini, or small chili peppers

1. Preheat the oven to 400°F (205°C) and line a baking sheet with parchment paper.
2. Cut out 3½- to 4-inch (9 to 10 cm) circles from the puff pastry. Add 1½ teaspoons of pizza sauce to the center of each circle, followed by a slice of pepperoni and 1 teaspoon of grated mozzarella cheese. Fold the round dough over the toppings securing at the top by pressing it all together and creating a ball, ensuring there are no openings.
3. Tie one 6-inch (15 cm) piece of butcher's twine around each dough ball, adding a knot at the seam, to create the pumpkin lines.
4. Place the balls with the seams down on the prepared baking sheet and place in the oven. Bake for 7 to 8 minutes, until golden brown. Let them cool before cutting and gently removing the string.
5. To make the stems: Use mini pepper stems for a natural look—simply pop them off the tops of chili peppers and press them into the pumpkin tops.
6. Serve warm.

TIP

Don't have peppers? Substitute with pretzel sticks, bamboo cocktail picks with twirly tops, or wooden cocktail picks with green frills. Get creative and use what you have on hand to make charming and unique stems.

BLACK COCOA MONSTER COOKIES

TOTAL TIME: 27 MINUTES **YIELD:** 15 TO 18 COOKIES

If you're an Oreo fan, you will be spellbound by these witchy cookies. The black cocoa powder not only creates the darkest cookie color, but it's also the secret ingredient that brings a complete Oreo dupe flavor to this recipe. But unlike Oreos, these cookies are chewy and rich, and the googly eyeballs soften into creamy chewy bits as well, making these as delicious as they are dark and spooky.

½ cup (1 stick, or 115 g) unsalted butter, softened
½ cup (110 g) packed light brown sugar
½ cup (100 g) granulated sugar
1 large egg
2 tablespoons 2 % milk
1 teaspoon vanilla extract
1 cup (120 g) all-purpose flour
½ cup (50 g) black cocoa powder
1 teaspoon baking soda
¼ teaspoon salt
1½ cups (260 g) semisweet chocolate chips
Candy eyeballs (such as Wilton)

1. Preheat the oven to 350°F (175°C) and line a baking sheet with parchment paper.
2. In a large bowl, mix the butter, brown and granulated sugars, egg, milk, and vanilla until well combined.
3. In a separate medium bowl, whisk together the flour, cocoa powder, baking soda, and salt.
4. Add the flour mixture to the butter mixture, stirring until well combined. Add the chocolate chips and mix again.
5. Scoop golf ball–size amounts of dough, roll them into balls, and place on the prepared baking sheet about 2 inches (5 cm) apart. Slightly press 8 to 10 candy eyeballs into the top and sides of each dough ball. This will seem like more than you feel is necessary, but the cookies will spread. You can also add more eyeballs to gaps as soon as they come out of the oven by pressing them into the cookies.
6. Bake for 10 to 12 minutes. Let them cool slightly for 3 to 5 minutes before transferring them to a rack to cool completely.

RECIPE

BLOODY JACK-O'-LANTERN HAND PIES

TOTAL TIME: 30 MINUTES **YIELD:** 4 SERVINGS

A warm and delicious—though totally creepy—hand pie is the perfect way to add a sweet finish to your spooky soirée. Your guests will goblin, ahem, I mean gobble them up with glee!

- 1 recipe Perfect Piecrust, chilled (see page 45)
- ¼ cup (60 ml) cherry pie filling
- 1 medium egg, well beaten, for the egg wash

1. Preheat the oven to 350°F (175°C) and line a baking sheet with parchment paper.
2. Place the chilled dough on a well-floured surface. Using a rolling pin, press down and roll outward to flatten the dough from the center to the edge, keeping the dough in place rather than stretching or dragging it forward, to avoid tearing. Lift and turn the dough 90 degrees each time you roll it out. Using a dough scraper or careful hands, re-flour the surface to prevent sticking. Repeat this process until the dough is a 12-inch (30.5 cm) circle.
3. Using a 3½-inch (9 cm) pumpkin-shaped cookie cutter, cut out 8 pumpkins from the dough. Place 4 of the pumpkins onto the prepared baking sheet and set aside.
4. With the next 4 pumpkins, cut faces into them. For a Jack Skellington–style design like you see here, cut out eyes shaped like tear drops tipped on their sides, poke two holes for the nose with a skewer or poker, and then cut a long smile without removing any of the dough.
5. Mash the cherry filling to make sure there are no lumps, then scoop a small spoonful of the filling onto each of the 4 uncut pumpkin crusts.
6. Place the jack-o'-lantern layer of dough on top of the bottom uncut pumpkin layer and secure around the sides by pressing around the outer seam of the pumpkins with a fork, ensuring there are no gaps.
7. In a small bowl, whisk together the egg and 1 tablespoon of water until well combined. Brush the dough with the egg wash, avoiding touching the filling as best you can. Bake for 12 to 15 minutes, until the edges begin to turn golden.
8. Let them cool for 5 minutes, and enjoy!

TIPS

You can use store-bought piecrust instead of homemade. The jack-o'-lantern faces makes this an excellent recipe to invite the kids to take part in making.

THANKSGIVING

There is no greater feeling than gratitude, and this holiday is a tribute to all the wondrous things we have, from the harvest to our loved ones. And what better way is there to feel lucky and grateful than to gather with family and friends over a meal prepared with love?

In my family, we whip up a variety of fun side dishes using many of our garden harvests to create a buffet-style spread from end to end on our kitchen island—the best recipes of which I'm about to share with you here! I hope that you love them and are inspired by them for your own yearly offerings, knowing that I am so grateful on this holiday to be sharing them with you.

On Thanksgiving, there is no focus on gifts, instead the focus is on a lot of great food, joy in abundance, and quirky traditions.

BOUNTIFUL BLESSINGS

The best thing about Thanksgiving is that it brings people together around a beautifully set table, not only to eat an amazing meal, but also to share stories and create memories. The dinner table becomes an integral part of making family and friends feel welcomed and cherished. As you prepare to gather around the table with your loved ones, it can be hard to figure out where to start, especially when you're hosting one of the year's biggest feasts. But don't worry—here are my tips for creating a welcoming Thanksgiving tablescape.

Florals

Thanksgiving is the perfect time to combine the freshness of fall flowers on your table with other warm elements. Here are a couple good ones to add to your table.

* **Hydrangeas**: These flowers represent gratitude and are available fresh and dried in abundance this season. When fully dried, white hydrangeas take on a lovely creamy and tan hue that is a perfect tone for the season.
* **Roses:** These flowers represent appreciation and gratitude and can be found in muted tones to coordinate with a subdued palette or in bright colors for a bold Thanksgiving look.
* **Sunflowers:** Sunflowers symbolize happiness and optimism, perfect for setting the tone for a Thanksgiving feast. Late-fall sunflowers come in beautiful, muted fall tones to fit the scene perfectly.
* **Asters:** These flowers symbolize patience and love, and as easy, long-lasting cut flowers, they are readily available in a variety of colors from floral retailers.

Colors

My Thanksgiving table inspiration started with my collection of wicker cornucopias. If you're like me and have found inspiration with one of this season's many elements and want it to shine through while still maintaining balance and a classic, traditional feeling, then you will want to choose more muted colors, such as:

* Warm taupe
* Soft sage green
* Beige
* Muted mustard yellow
* Light orange
* Brown

If you want to spice things up a bit and go for more vibrant fall hues, the following work great for giving your table a pop of color:

* Pumpkin orange
* Cranberry red
* Golden yellow

Integrating these bold colors with seasonal foliage like autumn leaves or berry branches, flowers, and seasonal fruits like pomegranates, apples, or pears will give your table a festive and dynamic look.

Centerpieces and Decor Suggestions

Picking pieces and accents to add around your table is especially fun during this season, as there are so many inspirational items to work with. You can use a large, earthy vase with a mixture of dried and fresh flowers and add accent pieces that symbolize Thanksgiving all around it.

Here are some additional Thanksgiving accents to enhance your tablescape and capture the warmth and gratitude of the season:

* **Mini pumpkins and gourds**: Use white, orange, or even metallic-painted mini pumpkins and gourds to add festive charm to each place setting or centerpiece.
* **Candles:** Incorporate a mix of taper, pillar, or tea-light candles in warm tones like gold, copper, or amber for a soft, glowing ambiance.
* **Thanksgiving-themed figurines**: Add small turkey figurines, acorn accents, or harvest-themed decor for a playful seasonal nod.

Tablecloth

Tablecloths and runners are an easy way to add texture, color, and warmth to your Thanksgiving tablescape. To create a warm, late-fall vibe, try using a large plaid wool pashmina scarf as a runner. For my table, I chose one in muted tones and placed it across the center widthwise, rather than the usual lengthwise direction, for a unique touch. If you'd like to achieve a similar look, you can use:

* **Solid tablecloths:** Thick-textured tablecloths or runners—like velvet or twill—add warmth and depth to your table. For an elegant Thanksgiving look, consider rich tones such as warm creams, tans, soft greens, mauves, or muted reds. If you want to go bolder but still want to keep it elegant, a velvet or satin tablecloth in a vivid hue like golden-yellow satin or cranberry-red velvet might be your ideal pick.
* **Patterned tablecloths:** Before Thanksgiving, all sorts of turkey prints, cornucopia prints, fall plaids, and leaf motifs will be available at local retailers, and you may find your perfect pattern to create a yearly Thanksgiving table tradition.
* **Scarves or blankets as table linens**: It is easy to find beautiful fall-toned plaids and softer textures in scarves and blankets, which you can use as layers creating cozy combinations for the essence of fall. As I mentioned before, you can use what you can find around the house, and let your imagination guide you to experiment with what might look great on your table.

Place Settings

Place settings play a vital role in creating a warm and inviting Thanksgiving tablescape. Layered textures, thoughtful details, and cohesive elements like copper-toned flatware and amber glassware set the tone for a memorable celebration. For your table, you will want to select place settings that complement your overall look without cluttering the design too much. To create your look, try the following:

* Opt for thick burlap, wooden, or woven place mats, or choose colored styles that complement your palette while adding plenty of texture.
* Stick to classic cream or white plates for a timeless look. For Thanksgiving, consider layering two to three plates or bowls of varying sizes, with the largest plate at the base for added elegance.
* Use your best cutlery in gold, copper, or stainless steel, ensuring it's polished to perfection.
* Incorporate classic accents like cornucopias, ceramic turkeys, or pumpkins to embrace the festive spirit.
* Include cute salt and pepper shakers and a butter dish for easy access at the table.
* Use cake stands or domes to display bread or other sides, adding height and visual interest.
* Add warm lighting with candles in wooden or metallic holders that coordinate with your cutlery.

Handmade with love
Handmade with love
Handmade with love

VANILLA EXTRACT GIFTABLE

This homemade vanilla extract is like bottling up a little bountiful flavor magic. It's the DIY gift that keeps on giving! As the extract ages, it only gets deeper and more complex in flavor, making it a delightful treat that will remind your recipient of your thoughtfulness long after the holiday season.

- 5-ounce (150 ml) empty bottles (such as Cholula hot sauce bottles)
- 6 vanilla beans per bottle (such as Tahitian or Madagascar)
- 4 to 5 ounces (150 ml to 180 ml) per bottle of high-quality rum, bourbon, vodka, or brandy
- Labels (store-bought or handmade)
- Gift tags
- Decorative tape (such as burlap)

1. Wash your bottles thoroughly with warm water and dish soap and allow to dry.
2. Slice the vanilla beans in half lengthwise. Insert one half-piece into each bottle. Fill the bottles with spirit of choice.
3. Add homemade labels handwritten on round paper stickers or store-bought labels from big-box craft stores to the front of your bottles. Add decorative tape around the tops, and tie gift tags to the vanilla bottles.
4. Store the bottles in a dark place such as a cabinet or pantry. Shake daily for the first week, then once every one or two weeks.
5. Vanilla extract is ready to use after a month, but it will be at its very best during months six to twelve.

ROASTED RED CABBAGE STEAKS

TOTAL TIME: 40 MINUTES **YIELD:** 6 STEAKS

I adore a colorful side dish, and when they say eat the rainbow, this recipe delivers on both vibrancy and taste. With simple ingredients and preparation, these cabbage steaks are a wonderful addition to a complex Thanksgiving spread. You'll be delighted when everyone oohs and ahhs over the brightness and fun they add to your spread!

- 1 large head red cabbage
- 4 tablespoons (60 ml) olive oil, divided
- 6 cloves garlic, crushed, plus more to taste
- 1 cup (100 g) finely shredded fresh Parmesan cheese
- 2 tablespoons finely chopped fresh dill or curly parsley
- Sea salt flakes (such as Maldon Sea Salt Flakes), to taste

1. Preheat the oven to 400°F (205°C) and line a baking sheet with parchment paper.
2. Peel away any tough outer leaves from the cabbage. Slice the cabbage into six ¾-inch-thick (2 cm) rounds, keeping the core intact to hold the slices together. Place the cabbage steaks on the prepared baking sheet. Brush each steak with olive oil, using about ½ tablespoon per steak.
3. In a small bowl, combine the remaining olive oil, garlic, and Parmesan cheese. Spoon 2 tablespoons of the garlic and Parmesan mixture to the top of each cabbage wedge and spread it evenly across.
4. Bake for about 20 minutes, depending on the thickness/toughness of the cabbage steaks. They should slice easily with a butter knife. Set your oven to high broil for the last 3 to 5 minutes, until the cheese is golden.
5. Garnish with fresh dill or parsley and sprinkle with sea salt to your liking.

RECIPE

PUFF PASTRY CORNUCOPIAS

TOTAL TIME: 35 MINUTES **YIELD:** 12 CORNUCOPIAS

For this adorable and theme-fitting appetizer, fast and fancy is name of the game. These cornucopias are so tasty and cute that no one will guess they were the easiest dish you made this Thanksgiving!

- 1 sheet (12-inch, or 30.5 cm) puff pastry, thawed
- 2 tablespoons finely chopped fresh parsley, plus 12 full leaves for garnish
- ½ cup (115 g) cream cheese, at room temperature

1. Preheat the oven to 375°F (190°C) and line a baking sheet with parchment paper.
2. Crumple up and shape some tinfoil into rough cornucopia cone shapes about 4 inches (10 cm) long and 1 inch (2.5 cm) thick at the opening.
3. Cut your puff pastry into twelve 1-inch-wide (2.5 cm) strips. Wrap the strips around the foil cornucopias, beginning at the center of the cones and working toward the tips to form pointed ends. Overlap the strips as you go. Place them on the parchment paper and bake for 10 to 15 minutes, until golden brown. Allow to cool, then slide off the foil.
4. In a medium bowl, mix the finely chopped parsley and the cream cheese until well combined. Using a piping bag with the large star tip, or fill a zip-top bag with the mix and cut a corner off, fill up the cornucopias with the cream cheese filling. Garnish each cornucopia with a parsley leaf. Arrange on a plate and serve!

TIPS

This is a great recipe to include your kids in the prep! Crafty kids will love doing the foil task.

You can also make the cornucopias using metal pastry cones instead of tinfoil and creating a twirly tail when wrapping the strips.

STOVETOP APPLE & BACON STUFFING

TOTAL TIME: 1 HOUR AND 15 MINUTES **YIELD:** 6 TO 8 SERVINGS

I have a confession to make when it comes to a Thanksgiving spread: Deep down inside, the only thing I am really thinking about is stuffing, and more specifically, this stuffing. Made with sweet apples and salty bacon, plus beer (the secret key ingredient) and butter, it's a staple side dish full of unique flavors that will have every stuffing lover asking for your recipe.

⅓ cup (75 g) salted butter, divided, plus 1 tablespoon softened for greasing
½ package (6 ounces, or 170 g) bacon, sliced fine
1 onion, finely diced
2 Gala apples or other tart apples, peeled and sliced into small cubes or matchsticks
1 tablespoon dried sage
6 cups (600 g) large dried/stale bread cubes
½ cup (120 ml) chicken broth
½ cup (120 ml) amber or dark beer
Salt and black pepper, to taste

1. Preheat the oven to 350°F (175°C) and generously grease a 9 × 9-inch (23 × 23 cm) baking dish with softened butter. Set aside.
2. In a medium skillet, cook the bacon over medium heat, flipping once, until crispy, about 8 minutes. Transfer to a paper towel–lined plate to soak up any extra grease.
3. In a sauté pan over medium-low heat, melt 3 tablespoons of butter. Add the onion and sauté until it starts to become translucent. Mix in the apples and the sage. Simmer over low heat for another 2 to 3 minutes. Remove from the heat. Allow the mixture to cool for about 5 minutes, until just warm.
4. In a large mixing bowl, add the dried bread cubes and pour the apple mixture over them, tossing until well combined. Slowly add the broth to the bread cubes, tossing to evenly distribute. Repeat this process with the beer. Taste the mixture and add salt and pepper to taste. Toss to ensure everything is well combined.
5. Transfer the stuffing mixture to the prepared baking dish. Cover the dish with a lid or foil and bake for 30 minutes. Fluff and turn over the stuffing. In the meantime, melt the remaining butter in the microwave for 10 to 15 seconds until fully liquefied. Brush the melted butter over the stuffing, then bake uncovered for an additional 15 minutes. For an extra-crispy top, turn the broiler on high for 1 or 2 minutes at the end of the cooking time.
6. Serve immediately, or set aside and and broil (see Step 5) just before serving.

RECIPE

HASSELBACK ROASTED CARROTS

TOTAL TIME: 1 HOUR AND 5 MINUTES **YIELD:** 6 SERVINGS

Anytime you have a root veggie to bake is a great time to use the Hasselback technique seen previously on page 119, as it will bring the maximum amount of flavor, inner softness, and outer crispiness to the vegetables in the dish. In this recipe, honey and butter infused with rosemary make it a perfect salty-sweet Thanksgiving vegetable side dish to complement all the savory offerings on the menu.

2 pounds (907 g) large carrots
½ cup (1 stick, or 115 g) unsalted butter
1 tablespoon rosemary
Salt and black pepper, to taste
2 tablespoons honey

1. Slice off the tops and very tips of the carrots. Working carefully, cut thin slices into them, levering the knife down through each carrot, stopping ¾ of the way down to make thin Hasselback cuts, ensuring not to cut all the whole way through. Continue cutting this way along the entire length of each carrot.
2. In a large pot over medium-high heat, blanch the carrots in salted boiling water for 3 minutes, then drain and allow to dry completely.
3. Preheat the oven to 355°F (180°C).
4. Transfer the carrots into an oven dish or Dutch oven, placing them in a single layer.
5. Melt the butter and pour it over the carrots, using a pastry brush to get it into the slits. Sprinkle the rosemary on top and season with salt and pepper.
6. Roast the carrots for 25 minutes, then baste again with the butter from the dish, and brush honey over the surface. Return to the oven for another 10 to 15 minutes, until cooked. Broil on high for 2 to 3 minutes, watching carefully to caramelize the tops without burning, if desired.
7. Serve hot!

RECIPE

ZUCCHINI APPLE BUNDT CAKE

TOTAL TIME: 1 HOUR AND 25 MINUTES **YIELD:** 1 BUNDT CAKE, 10 TO 12 SERVINGS

What better way to use up the ample and easily-stored harvests of zucchini and apple that fall offers than to make a rich, soft, and moist cake that is full of goodness? Even unfrosted, this Bundt cake looks delightful, giving you the option to add a little or a lot of frosting or leave it bare (making a great breakfast cake).

FOR THE CAKE

Unsalted butter, for greasing the pan
3 cups (360 g) all-purpose flour, plus more for dusting
3 large eggs
1½ cups (300 g) granulated sugar
1 cup (240 ml) avocado oil
1½ teaspoons ground cinnamon
½ teaspoon ground nutmeg
¼ teaspoon ground clove
1 teaspoon salt
1 teaspoon baking powder
1 teaspoon baking soda
2 cups (272 g) coarsely shredded zucchini
2 cups (320 g) apples, peeled, cored, and diced

FOR THE ICING

2 cups (240 g) confectioners' sugar
2 tablespoons 2% milk

1. Preheat the oven to 375°F (190°C). Grease the Bundt pan with butter and dust with flour.
2. In a large bowl, mix the eggs, sugar, and oil together.
3. In separate large bowl, blend together the flour, cinnamon, nutmeg, clove, salt, baking powder, and baking soda. Slowly stir together the dry ingredients and the wet ingredients, being careful not to overmix. Fold the zucchini and apples into the mixture until just combined.
4. Pour the batter into the prepared Bundt pan and bake for 55 to 65 minutes, until a toothpick or knife inserted comes out clean. Let it cool for 15 minutes inside the pan then transfer onto a cooling rack to cool completely.
5. To make the icing: In a medium bowl, combine the confectioners' sugar and milk. Drizzle or stripe the icing onto the top of the cake and serve.

TIP

You can use confectioners' sugar instead of icing or leave your cake bare for a delicious breakfast cake.

TIP

You can replace the Caesar seasoning salt for any of your choice.

CLASSIC CAESAR COCKTAIL

TOTAL TIME: 5 MINUTES **YIELD:** 1 SERVING

The Caesar cocktail is Canada's bolder answer to the Bloody Mary, with a creative blend of vodka, tangy Clamato juice, hot sauce, Worcestershire, and a salted rim. And if that wasn't enough, garnishes range from a simple lime wedge with crisp celery to crunchy dill pickles, pepperoncini, pepperoni, pickled asparagus spears, bacon, pickled beans, cherry tomatoes, olives, and more. There's no end to what you can add, making this drink one part appetizer and two parts fun. It's a drink that is as unexpected as it is delicious!

FOR THE COCKTAIL

1/2 cup (100 g) Caesar seasoning salt, for the rim of the glass
1 lime wedge
Ice cubes
1 ounce (30 ml) vodka or gin
½ teaspoon hot sauce (such as Tabasco), plus more to taste
1 teaspoon Worcestershire sauce, plus more to taste
¼ teaspoon salt, plus more to taste
¼ teaspoon black pepper, plus more to taste
1 cup (240 ml) tomato and clam broth cocktail juice (such as Motts Clamato Juice)

FOR GARNISH

2 cherry tomatoes
2 green olives
3 dill pickle slices
1 celery stick
1 pepperoni stick
1 lime wedge

1. In a small dish or bowl, add the Caesar seasoning salt. Rub the lime wedge along the rim of the glass to wet it, then twist the rim of the glass into the salt to coat completely.
2. Fill the glass halfway with ice, and add the vodka, hot sauce, Worcestershire sauce, salt, and pepper, being careful not to touch the seasoning salt on the rim of the glass.
3. Top with the Clamato juice.
4. Onto a pick, slide a tomato, followed by a pickle slice, olive, pickle slice, olive, pickle slice, and tomato. Rest it on the glass.
5. Garnish with a celery stick, pepperoni stick, and lime wedge. Before serving, be sure to squeeze the lime, plop it in, and use the celery to stir. Enjoy!

WINTER

Despite the temperatures, winter is a cherished, special season with its own pace and beauty. In my corner of the world, sunny but cold days with limited hours of daylight are offset by the coziest nights. From late afternoon, the evenings go on for hours with the snow reflecting the moon and all the holiday lights, creating the most magical outdoor scenes. Inside, winter's warm gatherings, set with festive decor and cozy fires, bring joy as we create memories with every bite, carol, gift, and craft. This is the time to reap the rewards of the work put in all year and to rest. It's also a time for reflection and planning for the year ahead, celebrating wins and moving past losses as we welcome a new beginning.

HOLIDAY COCKTAIL PARTY

When I think of the holidays, I think of cocktail parties. Guests arrive a little more dressed up, a little more joyed up, and with a fancied-up spirit and energy. I love setting up for a cocktail party, where no grand table or sit-down dinner are required. The mood and pace of the evening is relaxed, with small holiday bites arranged around the entertaining space, offering something to nibble on in multiple spots. Good conversation flows as holiday music plays in the background. One key piece to my holiday cocktail set-up is a bar cart!

CAYMUS-SUISUN
Le Vin

HOLIDAY BAR CART

Beginning in late October, bar carts start to make their appearance in home decor retailers in anticipation of the holiday season, making this the ideal time to go on the hunt for one to add to your entertaining arsenal. There are no strict rules for creating a holiday bar cart, but here you'll find my suggestions for creating your own at home. Don't forget to have some fun!

Holiday Bar Cart Essentials

Each year, I look forward to pushing out and setting up my bar cart for the holidays. If you don't have a spot for a bar cart in your home, you can set up a similar look and vibe on a cocktail side table, a bench, a spot on your counter, or even on a shelf, by gathering some of the following supplies. When styling a bar cart for the holidays, there are a few key elements I recommend:

* **A vase filled with**:
  * Sprigs of red or white faux-berry picks
  * Fresh or faux cedar branches
* **Accessories, such as:**
  * Candles
  * Twinkle lights
  * A plate or bowl with cocktail garnishes, such as rosemary, sliced oranges, and fresh cranberries
  * An ice bucket or champagne bucket over a tray with ice tongs
  * A bar tool set and cocktail shaker
  * Shot glass, or a few
  * A set of mule mugs
  * A set of champagne flutes
  * A set of cocktail glasses
  * A couple bottles of favorite spirits/wine

Bar Cart Setup

A holiday bar cart is all about thoughtful arrangement, adding a few design touches, and functionality. Once you've gathered your essentials, follow these tips to style it:

* Begin by dedicating certain areas of the cart to specific purposes. For instance, for the top shelf, add cocktail glasses, garnishes, and spirits for easy access. Reserve the bottom shelf for the ice bucket and extra bottles or glasses, neatly grouped for practicality.
* Arrange your larger items, such as vases, ice buckets, and wine bottles toward the back to create balance. Use tiered trays or risers if you want to elevate smaller items or create a more elegant vibe.
* Mix decorative elements with functional items. For example, surround your bowl of garnishes or glasses with candles or twinkle lights and sprigs of red or white faux-berry picks to create a warm glow.
* Use holiday-themed details like the cedar branches sparingly to not overwhelm the space.
* Be sure to keep frequently used items, like your shaker, bowl, glasses, or tongs, easily accessible and not buried under decorative elements or too close to any candles.
* Place the bar cart in a well-lit area or enhance it with warm lights strung along the cart's frame.

This simple setup will turn your bar cart into a holiday centerpiece, making it a standout feature in your holiday celebration.

PUFF PASTRY SPINACH PINWHEELS

TOTAL TIME: 25 MINUTES **YIELD:** 15 PINWHEELS

This easy and delicious appetizer is a Greek spanakopita–inspired recipe, only instead of phyllo pastry, puff pastry takes the wheel and rolls into delectable swirls. Featuring a blend of cheeses and a little kick of spice via red pepper flakes, this is sure to be a holiday finger-food party favorite!

½ cup (115 g) cream cheese, softened
½ cup (75 g) crumbled feta cheese
1 teaspoon dried basil
1 teaspoon garlic powder
1 teaspoon red pepper flakes
½ teaspoon salt, plus more to taste
½ teaspoon black pepper, plus more to taste
1 large egg, for egg wash
All-purpose flour, for dusting (optional)
1 sheet (12-inch, or 30.5 cm) puff pastry dough, thawed
1 package (10 ounces, or 280 g) frozen spinach, thawed and squeezed dry
1 cup (110 g) grated light mozzarella cheese

1. Preheat the oven to 350°F (175°C) and line a baking sheet with parchment paper.
2. In a medium bowl, stir together the softened cream cheese, feta cheese, basil, garlic powder, red pepper flakes, salt, and pepper until well combined.
3. In a small bowl, whisk together the egg and 2 tablespoons of water until well combined. Unroll the sheet of puff pastry onto a baking mat or lightly floured surface and brush with some of the egg wash.
4. Spread the cheese mixture into an even layer on the pastry sheet, leaving a ½-inch (12 mm) edge all around, then evenly spread the spinach over the cheese mixture. Sprinkle the mozzarella evenly over the spinach.
5. Starting with the long side, roll the puff pastry into a log, then brush the log with egg wash and sprinkle with salt and pepper. Using a serrated knife, cut the log into ¾-inch (2 cm) slices. Lay the rollups flat on the baking sheet, 1½ inches (4 cm) apart.
6. Bake the pinwheels for 10 to 15 minutes, until puffy and golden brown, with the cheese melted.
7. Remove the pinwheels from the oven and let cool on the baking sheet for 5 to 10 minutes. Serve and enjoy!

TIPS

If you have the time, you can wrap the puff pastry log in plastic wrap and chill for 30 minutes before slicing. This will help the spinach pinwheels hold their shape better. Otherwise, as soon as they come out of the oven you can quickly reshape any pinwheels that have come apart.

TIPS

You can make these lollipops up to 3 days before serving, just be sure to store them in an airtight container in the refrigerator. You can replace the minced parsley with ½ cup (30 g) of finely diced green onion, if preferred. You can also substitute the hazelnuts for pistachios, pecans, walnuts, or macadamia nuts, if desired.

CRANBERRY HAZELNUT GOAT CHEESE LOLLIPOPS

TOTAL TIME: 15 MINUTES **YIELD:** 18 TO 20 CHEESE BALLS

These aren't your kindergartener's holiday lollipops! Filled with creamy goat cheese and covered in a festive coat of warm cinnamon, buttery hazelnuts, sweet cranberries, and fresh parsley, these beauties will be a hit, as well as a conversation starter. Easy to whip up in about fifteen minutes, they can be made a day ahead, and they travel incredibly well, making them a great option when you need to bring an appetizer to impress!

- 1¼ cups (145 g) plain goat cheese, softened
- 1 cup (1 block, or 230 g) cream cheese, softened
- 2 teaspoons ground cinnamon
- 2 tablespoons honey
- 1½ cups (170 g) crushed hazelnuts (see Notes), divided
- 1½ cups (225 g) diced dried cranberries
- ½ cup (15 g) minced fresh parsley
- 18 to 20 pretzel sticks
- 3 to 4 large green onions, very thinly sliced lengthwise

1. In a large bowl using a hand mixer, or in a stand mixer, beat together the goat cheese, cream cheese, cinnamon, and honey until light and fluffy. Fold in ½ cup (55 g) crushed hazelnuts until combined.
2. Line a baking sheet with parchment paper. In the center of the parchment paper, hand-mix together the remaining 1 cup (115 g) crushed hazelnuts, the dried cranberries, and parsley, forming a mound.
3. Using a 2-tablespoon cookie scoop or a large spoon, scoop out one ball of cheese filling (about 2 tablespoons) and roll it in the mound of hazelnuts, cranberries, and parsley. Continue with the remaining cheese and coating.
4. Gently press a pretzel stick into each, and tie a 3- to 4-inch (7.5 to 10 cm) piece of thinly sliced green onion into a knot at its base.
5. Refrigerate cheeseballs until ready to serve.

NOTES

If my hazelnuts are whole, I like to use my large mortar and pestle to crush them! After crushing, I pour them into a sieve to separate the meal (the powdery part) from the chunky parts. I use the more finely ground nuts in the cheese balls and the chunks for the exterior.

TIP

If you want a darker-colored ginger beer, you can replace the brown sugar with 3 tablespoons of brown sugar and 2 tablespoons of light molasses.

RECIPE

HOMEMADE GINGER BEER

TOTAL TIME: 48 HOURS AND 20 MINUTES **YIELD:** 8 CUPS (2 L)

Ginger beer is often confused with ginger ale. However, the difference is enormous, both in flavor and because carbonated ginger ale doesn't sport any of the health benefits. And I promise, the difference in taste when you make those homemade holiday cocktails starring your own immune-system-boosting, probiotic ginger beer, is going to knock your Christmas stockings off! I'm ho-ho-hoping you'll try it!

- 1 tablespoon grated fresh ginger
- 5 tablespoons packed light or dark brown sugar
- Pinch of sea salt
- ½ cup (120 ml) fresh lemon juice
- ¾ teaspoon brewer's yeast
- 4 tablespoons granulated sugar or honey, plus more to taste

1. In a medium pot, bring grated ginger and 2 cups (480 ml) of water to a boil. Add brown sugar and a pinch of salt and cook until the sugar is dissolved, 3 to 4 minutes, stirring occasionally. Strain the liquid through a sieve covered with a few layers of cheesecloth into a large mixing bowl and squeeze well.
2. Add 6 cups (1.4 L) water, lemon juice, and brewer's yeast. Stir to dissolve, and pour into four 16-ounce (473 ml) flip-top bottles (or equivalent) using a funnel, then cap them.
3. Let it ferment at room temperature for 48 hours, then transfer to the fridge to slow the fermentation process. The process is complete once the mixture is fizzy. (See Notes.)
4. After fermenting, add 1 tablespoon of sugar or honey per 16-ounce (473 ml) bottle. To do this, pour a small amount of ginger beer into a cup, dissolve the sweetener in it, then pour it back into the bottle and shake gently. Be careful when opening directly after shaking!
5. Serve over ice or in your favorite ginger ale–based cocktail recipe.

NOTES

If the bottle isn't fizzy after 48 hours, allow another 24 to 48 hours to ferment; timing can depend on the ambient temperature and the activity in the yeast. Store the beer in flip-top or screw top bottles, either in two 32-ounce (1-liter) bottles or four 16-ounce (0.5 liter) bottles.

STUFFED CUCUMBER BITES

TOTAL TIME: 10 MINUTES **YIELD:** 24 BITES

If you only have 10 minutes to throw an appetizer together that looks like you spent more time on it than you did, tastes great, is super healthy, and even sports Christmas colors, then this is the recipe you are looking for.

- 1 package (5.3 ounces, or 150 g) spreadable gourmet garlic-herb cheese (such as Boursin)
- 2 to 3 tablespoons heavy cream, plus more if needed
- 3 English cucumbers, chilled
- 12 grape tomatoes, sliced in half lengthwise
- Coarse salt

1. In a small bowl, combine the cheese with the heavy cream and stir with a fork until fluffy and smooth. Add more cream if needed, until the mixture reaches a smooth consistency for piping. Transfer the mixture to a pastry bag fitted with a decorative tip.
2. Wash and dry the cucumbers, then peel the cucumber skin in strips, leaving green skin between each strip to create a striped effect. Slice the cucumbers into twenty-four ¾-inch-thick (2 cm) pieces.
3. Using a spoon, grapefruit spoon, or melon baller, gently scoop out the center of each slice and discard, leaving a bowl in the middle to hold the filling.
4. Arrange the slices on a serving platter, then pipe a swirl of the cheese mixture onto each slice. Top with tomato slices, and sprinkle with salt.
5. Serve immediately or refrigerate for 30 minutes before serving for crisp, cold cucumbers and firmer cheese.

TIP

You can replace the heavy cream with half-and-half.

CRANBERRY MOSCOW MULE

RECIPE

TOTAL TIME: UNDER 5 MINUTES **YIELD:** 1 CUP (240 ML)

This Cranberry Moscow Mule is the quintessential holiday cocktail. This festive drink is super easy to customize to turn it into a non-alcoholic version for the kids or teetotalers, making it perfect for holiday entertaining. Best of all, you can use your Homemade Ginger Beer (page 191) to make a feel-good drink complete with the health benefits of a naturally fermented beverage.

Ice cubes
2 tablespoons vodka
1 large lime, cut in half, divided
¼ cup (60 ml) cranberry juice
½ cup (120 ml) Homemade Ginger Beer (see page 191)
Rosemary sprigs, for garnish
Cranberries, for garnish

1. Fill a copper mug with ice. Add the vodka.
2. Cut the lime in half and set one piece aside. Squeeze the juice of the lime half (about 1 tablespoon) into the mug, then add the cranberry juice and pour the ginger beer on top. Stir well.
3. Cut the remaining lime into slices and use 1 or 2 slices to garnish the drink along with rosemary stalks and cranberries. Enjoy!

TIP

You can replace the vodka with any spirit of your choice.

CHRISTMAS

I love all the holidays, but Christmas is my favorite. It brings wonderful memories of family time and cherished traditions of gathering and food. The week of Christmas always fills me with love and appreciation for centuries-old human traditions.

I adore going over the top with holiday decor, starting with a Christmas tree and spreading decorations throughout the house. Holiday puzzles are a must, and I enjoy sending out invitations to share the Christmas joy. For me, cooking, baking, and crafting are central to the season, creating lasting memories. In my family, we have a tradition where my kids decorate gingerbread houses, which I photograph each year, capturing their growth and skill over time. A tradition can be started simply by deciding to do something one year and continuing to do it every year. Traditions, whether old or new, make the season truly special and full of joy.

They don't call it the most wonderful time of the year for nothing.

HOLLY JOLLY FEAST

At the heart of Christmas is a well-dressed dinner table where family and friends gather to enjoy a meal prepared with care and creativity. The table is adorned with festive decorations, and the aroma of delicious dishes fills the air. It's a time of celebration, joy, gratitude, and togetherness. Table decor is essential in creating a welcoming atmosphere, and especially important for this special season. Since the holidays—especially Christmas—are typically a big event in many homes, I've put together decor ideas for two different table setups: an elegant tablescape and a more relaxed, casual setting.

Flowers

Using flowers to decorate your Christmas table brings a fresh and vibrant touch to your holiday celebrations. Whether you prefer a traditional or more relaxed, nature-inspired setup, the right floral arrangement can set the perfect mood.

Formal and Traditional Floral Arrangements:

For a classic and festive look, opt for bold, rich colors and traditional holiday blooms. These flowers work wonderfully in formal centerpieces, garlands, or elegant vases:

* **Holly**: Its deep-green leaves and bright-red berries make this flower a perfectly on-theme Christmas touch.
* **Mistletoe**: The lighter-green leaves accented with white berries immediately spark thoughts of affection and look beautiful peeking out in a centerpiece.
* **Red poinsettias**: This holiday favorite, with its striking red and green foliage, instantly brings warmth and festivity.
* **Magnolia**: This gorgeous flower adds texture and a refined touch to any tablescape.
* **Cedar branches**: The perfect greenery for any traditional arrangement or centerpiece.

Modern and Relaxed Floral Arrangements:

For a more modern, rustic, or bohemian table setting, consider flowers and greenery that offer softer, more natural tones with an organic feel:

* **Terra-cotta–hued roses**: The perfect warm alternative to bright reds.
* **White ranunculus or anemones**: These delicate and romantic flowers work great in minimalist arrangements.
* **Pink poinsettias**: Bring a modern flair to a classic Christmas floral.
* **Dried eucalyptus**: Its silvery-green leaves add an airy, effortless elegance.
* **Norfolk pine:** A bright, feathery pine that pairs beautifully with a nontraditional theme.

Colors

When planning your Christmas colors for your dinner event, you can choose to go traditional or venture off the beaten snowy path with a palette that feels out of the gift box. As I usually entertain at the table more than once over the holiday season, I love to get creative and use both traditional and nontraditional styling to keep each event feeling fresh.

The following are some suggested palettes that I tend to use as my base for planning:

Traditional Colors

When we think traditional Christmas, we immediately think of the following colors, which lend themselves well to a formal holiday table and theme.

* **Red**: From bright ruby reds to berry tones, deep wine to burgundy, red is a quintessential Christmas color that adds vibrancy and brings on the spirit of holiday.
* **White:** From the snowy scenes that surround us to the perfect complement to reds, white is a key Christmas and winter accent, and looks serene on its own.
* **Deep or bright green:** Reminiscent of Christmas trees and the forest, green paired with red or white instantly sings with the joy of the season.

These three classic hues together will evoke a timeless holiday feel, bringing warmth and nostalgia to your table. If you want to create a traditional tablescape, incorporating these colors through table linens, candles, dinnerware, and floral arrangements will set the perfect festive tone. Pairing them with metallic accents like gold or silver can add a touch of elegance and sophistication.

Less-Traditional Colors

If you prefer a more earthy, modern, or understated take on holiday decor, consider incorporating nature-inspired tones that still feel cozy and festive. The following colors work beautifully for a more relaxed, rustic, or bohemian Christmas tablescape.

* **Sage green**: This color adds a soft organic, natural feel.
* **Terra-cotta**: This warm tone pairs beautifully with greenery and wooden elements.
* **Cream**: A soft, neutral base that keeps the tablescape light and elegant.
* **Taupe**: A subtle, sophisticated shade that adds warmth without overpowering the scene.
* **Soft pink**: An inviting hue that complements gold or brass accents beautifully.

To complete this less-traditional look, consider using wooden chargers, linen napkins, dried florals, and ceramic dinnerware for a cozy, nature-inspired feel. Adding soft candlelight and textured elements like rattan or woven place mats can further enhance the warmth and charm of your holiday table.

Centerpieces and Decor Suggestions

Seasonal flowers and foliage make the best decor and centerpieces for this time of year. Whether you prefer using foliage alone or combining it with flowers, both options work beautifully, but don't forget all the amazing additions, both real and faux, that you can include. Some great seasonal arrangements and centerpiece options include:

* Faux garlands
* Faux berry, holly, and mistletoe picks
* Faux eucalyptus
* Pine cones
* Magnolia leaves
* Bows and ribbons
* Faux pears and apples
* Clay and wooden bead garlands
* Dried citrus slices and garlands
* Christmas ornaments

For a classic festive look, go for a full, lush garland running down the table, made of a variety of pine, cedar, and magnolia leaves. Add red berries, poinsettias, mistletoe picks, and faux pears, plus gold or silver Christmas ornaments for a rich, elegant touch. Enhance the ambiance with taper candles in festive holders and twinkle lights woven through the greenery.

For a more understated, organic look, a simple eucalyptus and pine leaf runner creates a natural, effortless feel. Pair it with neutral candles, pine cones, and dried orange slices for a cozy, rustic vibe. Swap out bright reds for terra-cotta or deep-green accents and use ceramic or wooden candleholders to maintain a warm, earthy esthetic.

Both setups create a cozy and inviting Christmas table, perfect for gathering with loved ones!

Tablecloth

You really can't go wrong with a traditional table or a less-traditional table, as either option would set the stage for a festive celebration—it's just a matter of preference. However, there are certain tablecloths that will work best for each vibe you're trying to encapsulate this holiday season.

Traditional Tablecloth Options

If you are going for a traditional route, the following tablecloths would be ideal for you:

* Holiday-themed prints like a nutcracker pattern, Santa motif, or snowflake print
* Plaids in red and green
* Solid satin in gold, silver, or wine tones
* Botanical prints featuring poinsettias, holly, or mistletoe
* Red and white, or green and white, stripes
* Solid red, green, or white

One tip to keep in mind when selecting a printed tablecloth is that many of them have directional prints, like Christmas trees all facing the same way, meaning one side of the table will see the print upside down. You may want to triple-check the print is viewable from every direction if symmetry is important to you.

Less-Traditional Tablecloth Options

If you want to go more simple or simply less traditional, the following tablecloths will work well and still look thoughtful for the season:

* Neutral-colored linen in cream, tan, or beige
* Solid-color cottons in sage green or terra-cotta
* Simple pinstriped tablecloths in warm neutral tones
* Burlap added as a table runner
* Simple, tone-on-tone dotted tablecloths

Pairing together a neutral-colored linen tablecloth provides a versatile canvas for your Christmas decor to stand out. Burlap adds texture and a cozy Christmas vibe, while a solid-color cotton tablecloth is simple, versatile, and can complement any decor. Each of these types of tablecloths are great to add to any decor collection as they can be used for various occasions.

Place Settings

Traditional elements such as elegant and coordinated china, festive napkins, and classic flatware set the tone for a timeless celebration. Place-setting decor that is a little less traditional focuses on simplicity and the beauty of nature, rather than glitz and glamor. Think relaxed or cute holiday plates, simple coordinating neutral ceramics, natural textures like burlap, linen, and wood, all combined with muted, earthy tones and accents.

Another tip I love to employ when planning for a really eclectic or highly detailed holiday-themed table, is to gather all the supplies and decor that I'm considering and group them together on the table, laying greenery over my tablecloth selection with dishes and decor and cutlery so I can start to see the vision all together before I start laying it all out or buying florals.

DRIED CITRUS ORNAMENTS

This is a PSA for all you holiday craft-lovers: Anything can become an ornament simply by having a mini wooden clothespin hot-glued to the back! Take dried citrus for example! Dried citrus makes charming decorations when hung from twine, but they often spin or slide, making it challenging to position them facing forward where they look best. An easy solution is to add a mini clothespin to the fruit, which makes it possible to perfectly place and position them right where you want them. No more spinning or sliding! This cool craft makes twelve ornaments.

2 to 3 citrus fruits of choice
Hot glue
Hot glue gun
12 mini clothespins

1. Using a sharp knife or electric meat slicer, slice the citrus thinly, between ⅛ to ¼ inch (3 mm to 6 mm). Arrange the citrus on a baking rack/cooling rack and place it on a cookie sheet. This allows airflow all around the slices to help them dehydrate faster.
2. If you have a dehydrate setting on your oven, preheat it to 140°F (60°C). Bake the slices for 4 hours, turning them halfway to ensure they cook evenly. If you don't have a dehydrate setting on your oven, bake the slices at 170°F (77°C), turning them every 30 minutes. Browning is a real possibility at this temperature, so be sure to closely monitor the slices and leave the oven door slightly open to allow heat and humidity to escape.
3. Once the slices are dry, turn off the oven. Allow to fully cool and dry out completely in the oven, about 1 hour. Keep the oven door slightly open if you were using the bake setting.
4. Hot-glue a mini clothespin on one side of each dried citrus slice.
5. Hang your ornament and enjoy!

lila
dad
cade

HANDMADE CLAY GIFT TAG

This is another one of my favorite giftable, compostable, and inexpensive holiday crafts. These reusable gift tags are so quick and fun to make and cost around fifty cents each! Writing out gift tags has always been my least favorite part of gift wrapping, and I've also never been a fan of the fact that they are usually nonbiodegradable stickers that just end up in the trash. The wonderful part is that there are so many ways you can use these cute tags: You can save and reuse them each year, they can become a handmade gift, or work double duty as a handmade gift and place marker at the table.

1 tub (2.5 pounds, or 1 kg) air-dry clay (such as Crayola)
Rolling pin
Waxed paper
Knife
Brown paper gift tags with strings
Letter stamps (optional)
A sharp poker or skewer

1. With wet hands, knead a tennis ball–sized chunk of clay until your clay is smooth and soft.
2. Over waxed paper, roll the clay to just under a ¼-inch (6 mm) thickness.
3. Cut your clay into long strips slightly smaller than your paper tags are, then divide them again into small rectangles, slightly shorter than your tags are, and cut off two corners of one end to match your tags' shape. Make as many as you need, returning any unused clay to the tub.
4. Press your letter stamps into the clay tags or carve a name in with a poker or skewer.
5. Poke a hole in the clay at the string end big enough to fit the strings on your gift tags. Allow the clay to dry for 24 hours.
6. Place your clay gift tag over the paper tag aligning the hole and threading the string through to connect both, and voila!

TIPS

These tags can also be used as ornaments. When you're done with them, you can compost the entire tag. Most of the items needed for this craft can be found either at Michaels or local dollar stores. One tub of clay can make up to 40 tags.

MUSTARD CAVIAR

TOTAL TIME: 40 MINUTES **YIELD:** 1 ½ TO 2 CUPS (400 TO 530 G)

Mustard caviar (also known as pickled mustard seeds, but that's way less fun) adds slightly crunchy bursts of flavor, fun texture, and visual interest to so many dishes, as well as being a fantastic condiment! It also makes an excellent homemade gift when packaged into cute jars.

½ cup (120 ml) white wine vinegar
1 cup (240 ml) apple cider vinegar
½ cup (110 g) packed (light or dark) brown sugar
1 teaspoon salt
1 cup (200 g) yellow mustard seeds

1. In a small saucepan, combine the white wine vinegar, apple cider vinegar, 1 cup (240 ml) of water, brown sugar, and salt. Stir until all the ingredients dissolve, 1 to 2 minutes.
2. In a medium-small saucepan, add the mustard seeds and cover with water. Bring to a boil; let boil for 30 seconds. Remove from the heat and strain the seeds through a fine-mesh strainer. Return the seeds to the empty pan and repeat this step three additional times. This process removes the bitterness from the mustard seeds.
3. Transfer the blanched seeds to the pan with the brine. Bring to a boil over medium-high heat and, once boiling, quickly reduce the heat to a low simmer. Simmer for 15 to 20 minutes, or until most of the water has been absorbed and the seeds get puffy. If the seeds become too dry, add 1 tablespoon of water at a time.
4. Transfer the seeds to a clean glass container and allow them to cool for 15 to 20 minutes. Cover and refrigerate until ready to use.

TIPS

You can add any flavor varieties you like by stirring in any sauces into the seeds in the jars and allowing them to marinate for 24 to 48 hours. You can add hot sauce, salad dressings, or maple syrup to sweeten them up. You can add dill pickle brine to your jars, or you can change the brine by using a dill pickle brine while cooking or opt for any brine recipe you like! You can substitute the brown sugar with honey or maple syrup.

CHARCUTERWREATH

RECIPE

TOTAL TIME: 45 MINUTES **YIELD:** 8 TO 10 SERVINGS

A must-have item at a holiday gathering is a charcuterie board, and this wreath-shaped beauty is a conversation-worthy little ditty. A charcuterie board filled with delicious meats, cheeses, fruits, and nuts is the perfect way to keep snacky hands and bellies happy without ruining dinner!

1 small Brie cheese wheel
3 tablespoons fig jam
6 ounces (85 g) herb-garlic goat cheese
2 triangle slices (7 ounces, or 200 g) aged white cheddar cheese
8 slices large pepper salami
16 slices regular salami
4 slices prosciutto
9 slices artisanal baguette
3 clusters (10 to 20 grapes) green grapes
3 clusters (10 to 20 grapes) red grapes
15 baked crackers
3 Cranberry Hazelnut Goat Cheese balls (see page 189)
1 jar (9.5 ounces, or 269 g) pimento-stuffed olives
1 jar (9.5 ounces, or 269 g) garlic-stuffed olives
2 cups (260 g) pistachios
¼ cup (35 g) pine nuts
1 cup (140 g) dried cranberries
10 sprigs (15 g) fresh parsley
16 (8-inch, or 20 cm) fresh rosemary sprigs
2 large candy canes

1. Press a heart-shaped cookie cutter (or any shape of your choice) into the Brie and scoop out the shape. Fill the hole with fig jam.
2. Start assembling your board by placing the cheeses: Position the Brie at the top left, goat cheese slices at the top right, one cheddar triangle layered at the base of the goat cheese, and the last cheddar triangle at the bottom left.
3. Use the pepper salami and regular salami to make the 8-slice salami rosettes (see instructions on page 157). Place one pepper and one regular salami rosette under the goat cheese and sharp cheddar on the right. Tuck another regular salami rosette under the Brie. For variety, create a mix of folds and rosettes. Tuck one rolled slice of prosciutto under the rosettes, and place three more slices over the sharp cheddar on the bottom left.
4. Arrange the baguette slices in an arc over the goat cheese on the top right.
5. Add your fruits: Place one green grape cluster over the bread, one under the bread, and one between the salami and prosciutto on the bottom left. Tuck one red grape cluster above the Brie, one under the salami on the bottom right, and one at the bottom of the board.
6. Line up the crackers over the green grapes on the bottom left. Tuck 3 cheese balls under the crackers and grapes. Fill in the board with clusters of olives, nuts, dried cranberries, and additional crackers. Aim to maintain both a clear center and an outer circle, reserving some of each item for the finishing touches.
7. Slide parsley leaves under the board's perimeter to add a fresh, decorative touch. Add rosemary sprigs to the center in a circular shape and along the outline of the wreath, bending, sliding, and tucking them under the arrangement. Use any remaining olives, nuts, and dried cranberries to fill gaps. Tie two candy canes together in the shape of a heart with twine, and place them at the base of the board. Place the board for serving!

CRANBERRY MANDARIN BRUSSELS SPROUT SALAD

TOTAL TIME: 45 MINUTES **YIELD:** 4 TO 6 SERVINGS

The holidays are already so busy, and no one needs to spend too much time on another sophisticated side dish, so with just a few ingredients, this mandarin orange salad comes together quickly to add all the bright holiday colors to your festive menu—without so much work!

- 1 pound (454 g) Brussels sprouts
- 2 tablespoons olive oil
- 2 teaspoons garlic powder
- 1 teaspoon salt, plus more to taste
- 1 cup (240 ml) balsamic vinegar, for the balsamic glaze
- ¼ cup (60 ml) honey, for the balsamic glaze
- 3 mandarin oranges, peeled and segmented
- ¼ cup (35 g) dried cranberries
- ½ cup (65 g) toasted pine nuts
- ½ cup (55 g) sliced or slivered almonds

1. To roast the Brussels sprouts: Preheat the oven to 375°F (190°C) and line a baking sheet with parchment paper.
2. Trim the ends of the Brussels sprouts and remove any yellow leaves. Slice each Brussels sprout in half through the stem end. Place them in a medium bowl and toss with the olive oil, garlic powder, and salt.
3. Arrange the Brussels sprouts on the baking sheet, cut sides down. Roast for 20 to 25 minutes. For the last 5 to 10 minutes, flip them over for even browning until they are partially charred but not blackened. Add more salt to taste.
4. To make the balsamic glaze: In a medium pan, combine the balsamic vinegar and honey. Simmer over medium heat for 5 to 10 minutes, stirring regularly, until the mixture reduces by about half. It should be just thick enough to coat the back of a spoon.
5. To assemble the salad: In a large bowl or serving dish, add one layer of roasted Brussels sprouts, mandarins, and cranberries, then drizzle with ¼ cup (60 ml) of the balsamic glaze. Create a second layer of roasted Brussels sprouts, mandarins, and cranberries. Drizzle with another ¼ cup (60 ml) of the balsamic glaze.
6. Top with the toasted pine nuts and slivered almonds.
7. Drizzle with the remaining balsamic glaze before serving.

TIPS

You can replace the mandarins using 1 can (15 ounces, or 425 g) of canned mandarins. Also, feel free to replace the honey for ¼ cup (55 g) of light or dark brown sugar.

CITRUS, BEET & GOAT CHEESE GALETTE

TOTAL TIME: 45 MINUTES **YIELD:** 8 SERVINGS

A delightful twist on the classic savory tart, this galette makes a fantastic appetizer, side dish, or even a lunch main. No matter when I make it, it never lasts long! It's the most delicious way I've ever enjoyed beets, combining earthy, sweet, and tangy flavors that perfectly complement one another, in a dish as delicious as it is beautiful.

3 medium beets
Olive oil
1 recipe Perfect Piecrust, thawed (see page 45)
6 to 8 ounces (85 to 115 g) soft goat cheese, at room temperature, plus more for topping
⅓ cup (70 g) orange marmalade
1 large egg, for egg wash
Toasted pine nuts, for topping
Fresh thyme, for topping

1. Preheat the oven to 400°F (205°C). Wash the beets thoroughly, then cut off their tops and bottoms. Rub them with olive oil, wrap them individually in foil, and place on a rimmed baking sheet. Roast for 25 to 35 minutes. Allow to cool, then remove from the foil. Place them under cold water to remove their skin, and set aside.

2. Roll out the piecrust dough on a dusted surface to form a circle approximately 13 to 14 inches (33 cm to 35.5 cm) in diameter.

3. Preheat the oven to 425°F (220°C) and line a baking sheet with parchment paper.

4. Transfer the dough onto the baking sheet. Spread a layer of goat cheese on the dough, keeping 2 inches (5 cm) from the edges. Top the goat cheese with a layer of marmalade.

5. Slice the beets into ⅛-inch-thick (3 mm) round slices, then slice the rounds in half to create semicircles. Starting at the edge of the goat cheese and marmalade layer, arrange the semicircles with the rounded sides facing outward. Layer the beets over each other like flower petals, circling inward to the center, until the arrangement resembles a flower.

6. Fold the edges of the piecrust over the edge of the filling, creating a few folded pleats as you work around the galette. In a small bowl, whisk together the egg and 1 tablespoon of water until well combined. Brush the crust top with the egg wash.

7. Bake for 18 to 24 minutes, until the crust is golden brown. Remove from the oven and allow to cool for 5 minutes. Top with goat cheese, toasted pine nuts, and fresh thyme. Serve warm or at room temperature.

TIP

If you prefer, instead of buying your lamb already ground, you can opt to grind your own lamb meat in a stand mixer with a meat-grinder attachment.

RECIPE

CRANBERRY-MINT LAMB MEATBALLS

TOTAL TIME: 45 MINUTES **YIELD:** 16 TO 18 MEATBALLS

These lamb meatballs with cranberry sauce bring together Mediterranean warmth and festive flavors. Each golden-brown meatball is packed with garlic, fresh herbs, and a hint of cumin and coriander, making these aromatic, meaty bites an irresistible appetizer, side dish, or main course.

FOR THE MEATBALLS

1 small yellow onion, very finely diced
1 pound (454 g) ground lamb
3 to 5 cloves garlic, crushed
2 large eggs
½ cup (25 g) chopped fresh parsley, plus more for topping
½ cup (25 g) chopped mint leaves, plus more for topping
1 teaspoon ground cumin
1 teaspoon ground coriander
2 teaspoons kosher salt
½ teaspoon black pepper
⅔ cup (55 g) breadcrumbs (such as panko)
1 tablespoon olive oil

FOR THE GLAZE

⅓ cup (75 ml) balsamic vinegar
½ cup (120 ml) orange juice
½ cup (110 g) packed (light or dark) brown sugar
1 tablespoon cornstarch
1 cup (95 g) fresh cranberries, divided

1. To make the meatballs: In a medium bowl, use your hands to combine the onion, lamb, garlic, eggs, parsley, mint, cumin, coriander, salt, pepper, and breadcrumbs until well combined.
2. Using wet hands, roll the mixture into ping pong–sized balls (25 g each, about 1¾ inches or 4.5 cm diameter) and set aside. You should end up with 16 to 18 balls.
3. In a large skillet, heat the oil over medium heat for 3 to 5 minutes. Working in 2 to 3 batches to avoid overcrowding, brown the meatballs, giving the skillet a gentle shake occasionally to roll them around and let them cook evenly on each side. Once browned, reduce the heat to the lowest setting and cover the skillet. Cook the meatballs through for 2 to 3 minutes.
4. Place the meatballs in an ovenproof dish to keep warm.
5. To make the glaze: In a small saucepan, mix the balsamic vinegar, orange juice, and brown sugar together and bring to a simmer over medium-low or low heat. In a cup, mix together the cornstarch and ¾ cup (180 ml) of water, then pour the mixture into the pan. Add ⅔ cup (65 g) of the cranberries and continue to simmer until the sauce is sticky and the cranberries begin to burst. If the sauce gets too thick, add more water (about 2 tablespoons at a time). Remove from the heat and stir. Allow to cool slightly for 3 to 5 minutes.
6. In a medium serving dish, add the cranberry sauce and arrange the meatballs over the top, sprinkling with chopped mint, parsley, and the remaining cranberries. Serve and enjoy.

GARLIC DUCHESS POTATOES

TOTAL TIME: 1 HOUR AND 10 MINUTES **YIELD:** 12 SERVINGS

Duchess potatoes are a traditional French recipe that elevates regular mashed potatoes by combining mashed potatoes with egg yolks, butter, and seasonings to create delicate, crispy swirls. The only tricky part about this recipe is ensuring your mashed potatoes are as smooth as possible to be successful in the piping process.

3 pounds (1.3 k) Yukon gold potatoes, peeled and cubed
1 teaspoon salt, plus more to taste
¼ cup (½ stick, or 55 g) unsalted butter, softened
⅓ cup (75 ml) heavy cream
½ cup (50 g) grated Parmesan cheese, plus 2 tablespoons for sprinkling
1 teaspoon black pepper, plus more to taste
1 tablespoon garlic powder
3 large egg yolks
2 tablespoons unsalted butter, melted

1. In a large pot, add the cubed potatoes and enough cool water to cover them by 2 inches (5 cm). Add a pinch of salt and bring to a boil over medium-high heat. Reduce the heat to medium or medium-low, and simmer until the potatoes are just soft, about 15 minutes. Drain the potatoes well in a colander and let stand for 5 minutes.
2. Preheat the oven to 425°F (220°C). Line two baking sheets with parchment paper and spray with cooking spray.
3. In a large bowl, mash the potatoes well with a masher or pestle. Then, working in batches, pass the mashed potatoes through a fine-mesh sieve or food mill into a large bowl to ensure a silky texture. Use a spatula or wooden spoon to press the mash through, scraping the underside of the sieve as needed. Stir in the butter until melted and combined. Add the heavy cream, Parmesan cheese, 1 teaspoon salt, the pepper, and garlic powder. Adjust salt and pepper to taste. Add the egg yolks, one at a time, stirring until well incorporated. Transfer the potato mixture to a pastry bag with a large star tip, or a zip-top bag with the corner cut off.
4. Pipe 3-inch-round (7.5 cm) by 2-inch-high (5cm) potato swirls onto the prepared baking sheet, allowing 2 inches (5 cm) between swirls. You can make pretty lines in them with the tines of a fork or leave them as is. Freeze for 15 minutes, until firm to the touch.
5. Gently brush the potato swirls with melted butter and sprinkle with 2 tablespoons of Parmesan. Bake until the tops are golden and the centers are hot, about 20 minutes. Let stand for 2 to 3 minutes before transferring to a platter with a thin spatula. Serve hot.

TIPS

Yukon gold potatoes will yield the best and firmest piping results, followed by russet potatoes. Duchess potatoes can be piped and stored in the fridge a day in advance. Try not to overboil the potatoes or allow too much water to get into the mashing process, or the potatoes will not keep their shape in the oven.

TIP

You can gift these cookies in cellophane cookie bags or divide the dough and make other gingerbread shapes and types for a fun gingerbread cookie box!

RECIPE

GINGERBREAD COOKIE SANDWICHES

TOTAL TIME: 52 MINUTES **YIELD:** 24 COOKIES

I made these gingerbread cookies using a traditional wooden cookie mold in the shape of a pine cone, which results in a 3D cookie that looks dreamy. Gingerbread with cream cheese frosting makes the perfect flavor duo, and the holidays are the perfect time to venture out and make this a new favorite!

FOR THE COOKIES

4 cups (480 g) all-purpose flour, plus more as needed
1 teaspoon baking soda
1 teaspoon salt
1 cup (2 sticks, or 225 g) unsalted butter, softened
2 tablespoons grated fresh ginger
1 tablespoon ground cinnamon
1 teaspoon ground nutmeg
1 cup (200 g) granulated sugar
1 ¼ cups (300 ml) baking molasses
2 large eggs
Confectioners' sugar, for dusting

FOR THE FROSTING

1 cup (2 sticks, or 225 g) unsalted butter, softened
1 cup (230 g) cream cheese, softened
1 teaspoon Vanilla extract
1 bag (2.2 pounds, or 907 g) confectioners' sugar
1 drop green food coloring (optional)

1. To make the cookies: Line a baking sheet with parchment paper. In a medium bowl, sift together the flour, baking soda, and salt.
2. In a separate large bowl or in the bowl of a stand mixer fitted with a paddle attachment, mix the softened butter, ginger, cinnamon, nutmeg, and granulated sugar until well combined. Add the molasses and eggs and mix well. Add the flour mixture into the bowl ¾ cup (90 g) at a time until well combined. Add more flour as needed for a good, smooth, not-too-sticky consistency.
3. Spray the cookie mold with the cooking spray. Take a chunk of the dough large enough to roll it into a golf ball–sized ball and pat it with flour. Press the ball into the mold to create the pine cone shape, and tap it on a cutting board to release from the mold. Place the pine cone cookies on the prepared baking sheet, then freeze them for 10 minutes.
4. Preheat the oven to 375°F (190°C). Bake the cookies for 8 to 12 minutes. (For softer cookies, bake closer to 8 minutes and for crispier cookies, bake closer to 12 minutes.) Dust the cookies with confectioners' sugar while hot, then let them cool on a wire rack.
5. To make the frosting: In a stand mixer, whip together the butter and cream cheese until well combined. Add the vanilla. Bit by bit, add the confectioners' sugar, and whip together well. Add the drop of green food coloring, if desired, and whip for a few minutes, until well combined. Add the frosting to a piping bag.
6. Once the cookies have cooled, pipe the frosting thick onto the back of one pine cone and gently place another pine cone on top to create a sandwich. Serve and enjoy!

YULETIDE CARAMEL EGGNOG-SPIKED LATTE

TOTAL TIME: 5 MINUTES **YIELD:** 1 SERVING

One of my favorite traditions each year is scooping up a carton of eggnog the moment I see it hit the shelves, and switching out my morning latte milk for daily eggnog lattes—and here and there elevating them to cocktail status. Every warm sip of this latte is guaranteed to perk you up faster than Santa travels on Christmas Eve (wink, wink). With a swirl of dulce de leche, a dash of cinnamon spice, and a gingerbread garnish that's just too cute to eat (but you will), this festive treat is the best anytime during the season.

¾ cup (180 ml) eggnog
1 tablespoon dulce de leche or caramel sauce (such as Bonne Maman brand)
2 tablespoons rum-and-coffee liqueur (such as Kahlua)
2 tablespoons Irish cream (such as Bailey's)
1 cup (240 ml) hot brewed coffee
Ground cinnamon
Gingerbread cookie, for garnish (optional, see page 217)

1. Warm the eggnog using an electric milk frother, or microwave it and then froth it with a handheld frother until it reaches a foamy, latte-like consistency.
2. In a large (preferably clear) mug, use the back of a spoon to smear the dulce de leche around the inside walls of the mug. Add the rum-and-coffee liqueur and Irish cream, then pour in the brewed coffee, leaving 1 to 2 inches (2.5 to 5 cm) of space, depending on the size of your mug.
3. Fill to the top with the foamy, frothy, warm eggnog and sprinkle with the cinnamon.
4. Garnish with a cute gingerbread cookie, if desired.

NEW YEAR'S EVE

The end of the year brings with it a lot of emotions. Reflecting on the past can be beautiful and joyful or challenging, depending on our personal circumstances. However, there is always so much to reminisce about. This is why, I believe, we love to gather for New Year's Eve. It's always best enjoyed with a group of people who you can hug, shake hands with, kiss, and congratulate, recognizing that we all made it together to the gift of a new year as the clock strikes midnight.

As the last holiday of the year, it's such a special time to get a little sparkly, get a little wild, let loose, dance, and celebrate a fresh new start to come. It's also a time to celebrate all our new hopes and dreams for the upcoming year.

HAPPY
NEW YEAR
Kiss Me

NYE CHAMPAGNE BAR CART

The countdown is on and it's going to be a long night of fun, making this the perfect occasion for a champagne bar cart. It doesn't take much to transform your holiday bar cart into a welcome wagon full of festive decor and delicious, bubbly beverages just by adding a few key elements and a fun backdrop. When styling a bar cart for New Year's Eve, I love to stick with the classic scheme of gold, silver, crystal/glass, and black, with a touch of greenery.

This is a list of my favorite elements to add to a NYE bar cart:

NYE Bar Cart Essentials

* **A vase filled with**:
  * Seasonal greenery, like cedar branches
  * A few gold and/or silver floral picks
* A Happy New Year banner
* A garland or banner with gold and silver details
* Candles in gold or silver candleholders
* Bottles of water or sparkling water
* A gold or silver ice bucket or champagne bucket over a tray with ice tongs
* 1 to 2 champagnes of choice
* A set or two of champagne flutes
* A set or two of cocktail glasses
* A cocktail shaker and bar tool set
* A small clock on the cart or mounted on the wall behind it
* Coordinating helium balloons in black, gold, silver, clear, or white, tied to the cart, or regular filled balloons around the cart
* NYE–themed party favors as decor

Bar Cart Setup

Creating a festive and functional NYE bar cart setup is a perfect way to set the tone for the evening while making it easy for guests to help themselves. Here's a guide to help you design a stunning and practical bar cart for your celebration:

* Choose a gold, silver, black, or glass color scheme to bring elegance and festivity to your setup.
* Enhance the display by scattering balloons on the floor around the cart.
* Position the bar cart near you to welcome guests with a convenient self-serve beverage station.
* Monitor the cart throughout the evening to refill glasses and restock champagne or water bottles as needed.
* If you've planned a signature cocktail, consider setting it up for guests to prepare themselves and displaying it in a stylish glass dispenser for easy serving.
* Arrange items to fit your cart's space and add a creative touch to make it uniquely yours!

By thoughtfully curating your NYE bar cart, you can not only impress your guests but also create a smooth-flowing beverage station that adds both style and functionality to your celebration. Let your personality shine through the details, and have fun!

Kiss Me

NEW YEAR'S INTENTIONS TREE

If you are looking for a fun, easy, and inspiring addition to your New Year's Eve party, you might love this play on New Year's resolutions! This is a yearly tradition that one of my best friends and I started many years ago. Instead of making resolutions, which can sometimes feel negative, choose three positive keywords to inspire you to focus on the areas in your life that matter most, such as gratitude, peace, focus, strength, etc. For this activity and craft, I'm showing you how to create a tree so that you and your loved ones can add your intentions into the branches via gold and black stars. This is one tradition the whole family will love!

6 to 8 branches with lots of spaces to hang stars on them, either from outside or store-bought
Gold spray paint
1 floral foam, cut to vase size
1 large, heavy vase
1 pack of tissue paper, to shred and decoratively fill the vase
Fairy lights (battery-operated), optional
Scissors
1 pack gold cardstock paper
1 pack black cardstock paper
Star-shaped paper punch
Hole punch
1 spool thin ribbon in your choice of color
Gold or black Sharpie pen

1. Gather the branches for your arrangement, and spray-paint them with gold spray paint. Allow to dry and off-gas a couple days in advance.
2. Add the foam to your vase, using a serrated knife to cut it to size as needed, ensuring the vase is heavy enough not to tip; you can add pebbles to weigh it down before adding foam.
3. Insert the branches into the foam to create the "tree." Cover the bottom of the branches in the vase with shredded tissue, then arrange the fairy lights on and around the branches if desired.
4. Cut out or punch out 2-inch (5 cm) stars from gold cardstock and poke or punch a hole at the top of each. Insert ribbons through the holes in the stars to make hangers. Place the stars in an accessible and visible location. Make enough to accommodate the number of participants.
5. For the activity: Everyone is instructed to pick two to three words to inspire their next year, then write their name and the words on a star to hang on a branch. Once everyone has had a chance to add theirs, you can choose a time for everyone to pick stars from the tree and ask the participant to share the meaning and hopes behind their words.

GLITTERY BLACKBERRY GOAT CHEESE PHYLLO CUPS

TOTAL TIME: 30 MINUTES **YIELD:** 12 SERVINGS

All that glitters is gold with this appetizer that arrives on the New Year's Eve table dressed to impress! Shimmering, sugar-coated blackberries that sparkle like jewels, paired with tangy goat cheese and a dollop of homemade blackberry sauce come together in a flaky treat that's equal parts snazzy and snackable. Serving these beauties to ring in the year is a small bite your guests will *berry* much enjoy!

4 phyllo dough sheets (9 x 14-inch, or 23 cm x 36 cm), thawed
3 tablespoons unsalted butter, melted
2 cups (280 g) fresh blackberries, divided
¼ cup (50 g) sanding sugar
½ teaspoon edible gold glitter
Juice of ½ lemon
2 tablespoons honey
⅝ cup (70 g) goat cheese, at room temperature

1. Preheat the oven to 350°F (175°C).
2. Lay 1 phyllo dough sheet on a cutting board and brush with melted butter. Stack and brush the next 3 sheets on top of each other. Using a pizza cutter, cut the stack through all the sheets making 12 squares, then nestle each into a cup in a 12-cup muffin pan. Bake for 10 minutes, until golden brown. Remove and allow to cool on a rack.
3. Wash and gently pat dry 12 blackberries on a paper towel. In a small bowl, add the sanding sugar and edible gold glitter. Stir until well combined. Add the blackberries to the bowl, using a spoon to turn to coat. If the sugar is not sticking, add a spritz of water onto the blackberries and try again.
4. To make the blackberry sauce: In a small saucepan, simmer the remaining blackberries with the lemon juice and honey over medium heat until the berries begin to melt into a sauce. You can use a fork or spoon to break them up. Once they have rendered down into a jam-like mixture, about 10 minutes, remove from the heat. Press the mixture through a fine-mesh sieve to create a thick syrup.
5. To assemble the cups: Add 2 teaspoons of goat cheese into each phyllo cup. Add a drizzle of blackberry sauce and top with a glittery blackberry.

TIP

If you have any berries or sugar left over, use them to make a few extra glittery blackberries for cocktails cocktails (see recipe on page 233).

BAKED BRIE WITH FIG JAM

TOTAL TIME: 30 MINUTES **YIELD:** 12 SERVINGS

We are getting figgy with it with this festive baked Brie! Wrapped in golden puff pastry and topped with sweet fig jam, this gooey Brie, crowned with toasted pine nuts, honey, and a sprinkle of thyme, is built to be a crowd-pleaser. Topped with sliced figs and served with a warm artisanal baguette, it's a filling appetizer that pairs well with bubbly champagne at an elegant or cozy NYE soiree!

1 large egg, well beaten, for egg wash
All-purpose flour, for dusting (optional)
1 (10 x 12-inch, or 25 x 30 cm) sheet puff pastry, thawed
1 (16-ounce, or 453 g) Brie cheese wheel
½ cup (120 ml) fig jam
Honey, for topping
Toasted pine nuts, for topping
Fresh thyme, chopped, for topping
Fresh figs, for topping (optional)
Sliced artisanal baguette, for serving

1. Preheat the oven to 400°F (205°C) and line a baking sheet with parchment paper.
2. In a small bowl, beat the egg with 1 tablespoon of water to make the egg wash and set aside.
3. On a baking mat or lightly floured surface, roll out the puff pastry so it's slightly thin, keeping it mostly square-shaped. Put the puff pastry on the baking sheet, placing the wheel of Brie in the center.
4. Use a butter knife to create punctures halfway down into the Brie across the whole top. This allows the jam to penetrate the soft part of the cheese. Spread the fig jam on top of the Brie, then brush the egg wash along the inside of the pastry. Fold the pastry upward, making overlapping folds, to enclose the Brie, gently pressing on the seams to seal, with some of the fig jam exposed.
5. Brush the egg wash on the top and outside of the pastry and bake for 25 minutes, until the puff pastry is golden brown.
6. Remove from the oven and top the Brie with a drizzle of honey, followed by toasted pine nuts, chopped thyme, and fresh figs, if desired.
7. Serve on a platter surrounded by the sliced baguette.

RECIPE

SHRIMP WONTON CUPS

TOTAL TIME: 30 MINUTES **YIELD:** 24 SERVINGS

A little seafood is always a great addition for any New Year's appetizer spread, and these crispy wonton cups with a savory filling of shrimp, cheese, and veggies bring the perfect mix of creamy and crunch. You might say they're *shrimply* irresistible.

24 wonton wrappers
Cooking spray
10 ounces (284 g) shrimp, shelled, deveined, and cooked
½ cup (115 g) cream cheese, softened
1 clove garlic, minced
½ tablespoon Worcestershire sauce
2 medium green onions, finely chopped
⅓ cup (35 g) grated carrot
½ cup (55 g) shredded mozzarella cheese

1. Preheat the oven to 350°F (175°C).
2. Press the wonton wrappers into the cups of a mini muffin or cupcake pan. Lightly spray the wrappers with cooking spray and bake for 8 minutes. Remove the pan from the oven.
3. Chop the cooked shrimp into small ⅛- to ¼-inch (3 to 6 mm) crumble-type pieces. In a large bowl, mix the shrimp, cream cheese, garlic, Worcestershire sauce, green onions, carrot, and mozzarella until well combined.
4. Fill each wonton cup with about 1 tablespoon of the shrimp filling. Return to the oven for 7 additional minutes, or until the filling is bubbly. Serve immediately.

SPARKLING BLACKBERRY CHAMPAGNE MULES

TOTAL TIME: 10 MINUTES **YIELD:** 2 SERVINGS

You will be ready to ring in the New Year with this stunning, sparkly cocktail in hand. Featuring shimmery glittery blackberries and a hint of mint, it's a simple, elegant signature drink that will have you looking like a bartender extraordinaire, and is perfect for that strike-of-12 toast!

4 to 6 blackberries, divided
3 mint sprigs, divided
1 tablespoon fresh lemon juice
2 ounces (60 ml) vodka of choice
Ice cubes
1 cup (240 ml) sparkling water or carbonated drink of choice
1 cup (240 ml) champagne
¼ cup (50 g) sanding sugar
½ teaspoon edible gold glitter

1. In a shaker, muddle 2 of the blackberries, leaves of 1 mint sprig, and the lemon juice. Add the vodka and stir to combine. Strain the mixture equally into 2 glasses filled half-full with ice.
2. Top with sparkling water or carbonated beverage of choice, leaving an inch or two of room, and finish up with a splash of champagne.
3. Combine the sanding sugar and edible glitter in a small bowl. Toss the remaining blackberries in the sugar-glitter.
4. Using a cocktail pick, place 1 to 2 glittery blackberries across each glass. Garnish with a mint sprig and serve.

TIPS

If you would like to make this into a pitcher one day in advance, quadruple the recipe in a shaker and strain into a pitcher. You can also premake the glittery blackberries and store in a paper towel–lined sealed container in the fridge. You can replace the sparkling water with the Homemade Ginger Beer from page 191 for a fun flavor twist!

VALENTINES DAY

Valentine's Day is one of the most lighthearted holidays we get to celebrate, and it's the last holiday in the deep dark winter, coming in hot like a beacon of pink and red light! Even though it was traditionally a day for couples, now it's the perfect day to spend together with anyone you love (or anyone you might need to reward with chocolate)!

On this holiday, you can let your unapologetically mushy side shine without shame. Your day can include exchanging cute "I love you!" notes with your kids or other loved ones, eating amazing treats, sharing gifts, celebrating Galentine's with a sweet sip, and sharing a loving meal with your soulmate.

The beauty of Valentine's Day is that it makes room for love in all its incarnations, like one big heart-shaped permission slip, to get cheesy and celebrate unabashedly all the people who make life a little sweeter.

LOVEBIRD FIRESIDE PICNIC

What could make a better date for your favorite Valentine than a cute living room or sunroom fireside picnic for two? No fireplace? No problem! Use a portable electric fireplace or pop a fireplace video on your TV. This is one idea that's sure to melt the winter chill.

Florals

The go-to flowers for this holiday are roses, without question, and these are the perfect choice if you're going for traditional. However, below are my suggestions of other flowers that work beautifully and will be available in February.

* **Lilies:** Oriental and Asiatic lilies make the ideal Valentine flowers, particularly in pink and white. Pink lilies, in particular, symbolize admiration.
* **Baby's breath:** This dainty, white floral looks stunning when overflowing in a vase or paired with other flowers. It represents purity and everlasting love.
* **Orchids:** For a unique option, consider potted orchids. They add flair to your table while symbolizing love and beauty.
* **Faux plants/potted plants:** If you prefer a fuss-free alternative, opt for potted plants or faux plants. Place them in charming red ceramic pots to dress up your table.

Colors

For Valentine's Day, choosing the right colors for a cozy picnic setup is easy, as there are three main colors that show off the love this holiday, which include:

* Red
* White
* Pink

But if you want to go off the beaten path and add a touch of elegance, or if you want to go against the grain a bit and do something different, you can opt for colors like gold and lavender. Lavender also provides a soft and romantic touch, and gold is the go-to color for adding a little glamour to your table setup.

Centerpieces and Decor Suggestions

There are a few ways you could go about playing around with colors and choosing the right centerpiece for a Valentine's Day setup. However, you want to be sure that whatever you choose does not block the view between you and your partner or disturb the simplicity of the picnic. You can add to a simple setup with:

* Small vases in white or red or glass, filled with your selected flowers
* Cute accent pieces around the vase and table, like heart-shaped decor or sweet treats
* Scattered candles in your chosen color scheme also work wonderfully to set the romantic mood
* Personal touches like framed photos or keepsakes
* A table topped with or surrounded by fairy lights can give your scene a more whimsical mood

For my setup, I used a portable picnic table, which I also used for my Tea for Two Picnic setup (see page 85), and I opted for a large red-and-white striped tablecloth as my base layer. If you don't have a portable or small table, you can always use a beautiful blanket set out on the floor. A couple of blankets that I recommend include:

* **Faux fur blanket:** This blanket is incredibly soft and adds a luxury feel to your setup.
* **Quilt:** This style is cozy and brings a sense of warmth, perfect in front of the fireplace.
* **Patterned:** This type of blanket is great to use if you want to have some fun with your decor. Think hearts, flowers, and more.
* **Additional blankets:** You can also add a couple more blankets of various designs or colors and pillows to the scene to create some layered softness.

I also suggest adding some round pillows for seating as they are great for comfort while also being stylish. You can also add some square throw pillows within your color scheme.

When adding blankets and pillows, I recommend shopping your home first, using what you have available, or add some new coordinating pillow covers—anything new you can keep and reuse each year.

Place Settings

Creating a romantic and cohesive table setting for Valentine's Day is all about balancing colors and adding thoughtful touches to enhance the atmosphere. For my table, I chose a traditional red-and-white theme with cream as an accent. I used red and white stripes on the table and featured simple white dishes layered with cream napkins, secured by elegant cream floral napkin rings.

Ideally, for a look like this, you want to opt for place settings that balance out your chosen colors and visually link them together. For example, if you prefer pink and white over red, a great combination might include pink place mats paired with white dishes. To add to the romantic scene, you can also add champagne flutes and even add patterned cups, like heart-shaped mugs.

If you'd like to incorporate purple and gold into your Valentine's Day place settings, here's how you can make it work.

* Make sure you have color balance. Use purple and gold as your primary accents while complementing with neutral tones like white or cream, such as white or cream plates to keep the look elegant.
* Start with adding gold place mats or chargers to create a luxurious base.
* Incorporate lavender napkins or if you don't have lavender napkins, use napkin rings for a pop of color that ties the theme together.
* Use lavender-themed glassware/mugs or champagne flutes with gold rims for a refined touch.
* Add small decorative details like gold flatware or lavender votive candles.
* Use a lavender table runner or cloth to bring in the color without overwhelming the table.
* Complement the settings with lavender-colored flowers, like orchids or lilies, mixed with golden accents (like gold-sprayed baby's breath).

TIPS

You can use stamps or toothpicks to add designs into the clay, such as words. You can also decorate the clay with any natural leaves, etc.

PRESSED FLOWER–HEART SEED BOMBS

Let's grow some love! Seed bombs, which are small bundles of seeds mixed within clay or paper, began as an ancient Japanese practice, reintroduced in the 1930s by a man named Masanobu Fukuoka. He seed-bombed on riverbanks, roadsides, and wasteland, allowing the seeds to grow up with the weeds. He believed that vegetables and flowers grown in this way were under Mother Nature's care.

Later, in New York during the 1970s, "guerilla gardeners" launched seed bombs made from all sorts of vessels, anywhere cracks and soil were found, aiming to bring green life back to the city. And now, here I am bringing you this easy and fun craft so you can make these seed bomb valentines for your kids to pass along, make at a Galentine's day craft night, make for wedding favors, or share as a gift with a friend!

1 Natural Earth air-dry clay tube (such as Craft Smart)
1 bag (5 pounds, or 2.3 k) soil or compost
1 bag (4 to 5 ounces, or 115 g to 412 g) wildflower seeds (such as McKenzie or Burpees) or native seeds from your area
Paint brush
Pressed flowers (optional)
Dried petals (optional)

1. Scoop out a ball of air-dry clay, about 2 tablespoons. Using your fingers and thumb, squish it in the palm of your hand, creating a flat, round disk about 2½ inches (6 cm) in diameter and ¼ inch (6 mm) thick. Place the soil in a little mound in the middle of the disk and add the wildflower seeds on top of the soil. Fold the edges in toward the center over the soil and seeds, sealing them at the top, then shape the ball into a heart. Add a little water to your fingers to make sure it is all smooth and sealed.
2. Using a paint brush dipped in water, brush the top of the heart to moisten and then press your dried flowers and petals (if using) into the clay. Repeat with the remaining clay, soil, seeds, and flowers.
3. Toss the heart seed bombs anywhere there is a chance for them to grow in the spring or rainy season. It is important to place them in a wet location so that the clay absorbs water, allowing the seeds to germinate, and then melts away as they grow.

NOTES

I used a drought-tolerant wildflower seed mix of native plants from Manitoba, so they have a great chance at life. But if the wildflower seeds you use aren't invasive, you can pretty much use any you like! 1 pound (453 g) of clay will make approximately 12 seed bombs.

STRAWBERRY SURPRISE HEART LOAF CAKE

TOTAL TIME: 2 ½ HOURS **YIELD:** 8 SERVINGS

Now, a Valentine's cake on its own is pretty incredible. But a pretty Valentine's cake that reveals a bright red strawberry heart-shaped center when it's sliced makes this a love-day cake to be remembered! Drizzled with creamy vanilla icing and topped with chocolate-dipped strawberry hearts, this cake is sure to win the love of anyone who has the joy of cutting a piece!

FOR THE CENTER HEART

1 cup (2 sticks, or 225 g) unsalted butter, softened

1 ¼ cups (250 g) granulated sugar

3 large eggs

1 teaspoon strawberry extract (such as Watkins)

½ teaspoon red or pink food coloring

2 cups (240 g) all-purpose flour

1 teaspoon baking powder

FOR THE VANILLA CAKE

1 ¼ cups (2 ½ sticks, or 280 g) unsalted butter, softened

1½ cups (300 g) granulated sugar

4 large eggs

1 teaspoon vanilla extract

2 ⅓ cups (280 g) all-purpose flour

½ teaspoon baking powder

FOR THE ICING

1 ¼ cups (150 g) confectioners' sugar

2 tablespoons 2 % milk

1 teaspoon vanilla extract

FOR THE TOPPER

4 to 6 strawberries

1 cup (300 g) white chocolate melting wafers

1. To make the red cake hearts: Preheat the oven to 350°F (175°C) and line an 8 × 4 × 3-inch (20 × 10 × 8 cm) loaf tin with parchment paper.
2. In a large bowl or in a stand mixer fitted with a paddle attachment, cream the butter and sugar together until well combined and fluffy. Add the eggs and mix well until fully combined, scraping down the sides of the bowl as needed. Add the strawberry extract and food coloring and mix well. In a separate medium bowl, whisk the flour and baking powder until well mixed. Fold the wet ingredients into the dry ingredients with a spatula until fully combined.
3. Pour the batter into the prepared loaf tin and bake for 45 to 50 minutes, until a skewer or toothpick inserted comes out clean. Remove from the oven, and let it rest for 10 minutes. Transfer onto a baking rack and allow to cool fully for about 1 hour.
4. Slice the loaf into seven to eight 2½-inch-thick (6 cm) slices. Use a 2½-inch (6 cm) cookie cutter to cut out a heart shape from each slice and set aside. Eat, discard, or save the scraps.
5. To make the vanilla cake with heart center: Preheat the oven to 350°F (175°C) and line an 8 × 4 × 3-inch (20 × 10 × 8 cm) loaf tin with parchment paper.
6. In a large bowl or in a stand mixer fitted with a paddle attachment, cream the butter and sugar together until well combined and fluffy. Add the eggs and vanilla and mix well until fully combined, scraping down the sides of the bowl as needed. In a separate medium bowl, whisk the flour and baking powder until well mixed. Fold the wet ingredients into the dry ingredients until fully combined.
7. Pour 1 to 1½ inches (2.4 cm to 4 cm) of vanilla batter onto the bottom of the prepared loaf tin, then place the red hearts standing pointy side down in the batter, each one snug and tight next to the other in a row down the middle of the loaf tin, leaving room on each end to hide the hearts. Place the remaining batter into a piping bag and pipe it into all the nooks and crannies around the hearts until the hearts are no longer visible. Gently place in the oven and bake for 45 to 55 minutes. Allow to cool fully before decorating.
8. To make the icing: In a large measuring cup with a spout, mix the confectioners' sugar, 1 tablespoon of the milk, and the vanilla until well combined. Add the remaining tablespoon of milk slowly, mixing until you have a thick icing. Pour the icing across the top of the cake, using the back of a spoon to encourage the icing to drip over the sides if needed.
9. To make the chocolate-dipped strawberry toppers: Wash the strawberries and cut out a v in the top center to create the heart shape, then pat dry. Microwave the white chocolate wafers in a microwave-safe bowl for 45 seconds. Stir, then microwave again for 30 seconds, stirring well until completely melted. Dip the heart tops of the strawberries into the melted white chocolate, then place on your cake as you like.
10. Serve immediately or within 24 hours.

RECIPE

TIPS

For making ahead, make the complete cake with icing and decorated strawberries, and store in an airtight container in the fridge for up to 3 days, or premake the cake only and freeze for up to 3 months in a sealed freezer bag. Allow to defrost at room temperature before icing as directed.

HEART-FILLED FOCACCIA

TOTAL TIME: 5 HOURS AND 30 MINUTES **YIELD:** ONE 9 × 13-INCH (23 × 33CM) FOCACCIA LOAF

If you are looking for a way into a bread-lover's heart, this focaccia is your route. Chewy, pillowy, salty goodness awaits, and all those who are invited to partake will surely be exclaiming, "You stole my focheartccia!"

FOR THE FOCACCIA DOUGH

1 ¾ cups (420 ml) warm water
1 teaspoon yeast
1 teaspoon honey
2 tablespoons olive oil, divided, plus more for greasing
2 teaspoons salt
4 cups (480 g) all-purpose flour

FOR THE TOPPING

12 grape tomatoes, washed and dried
½ cup (50 g) shredded Parmesan cheese
½ cup (55 g) shredded mozzarella cheese
¼ cup (20 g) fresh whole rosemary leaves
1 teaspoon flake or coarse salt, for sprinkling

1. To make the focaccia: In a large mixing bowl, use a spoon to stir together the warm water, yeast, honey, 1 tablespoon olive oil, and the salt until well combined. Add the flour and combine until a craggy dough forms. Cover the bowl with a beeswax cover, plastic wrap, or tea towel and set aside in a warm place for 15 minutes.

2. Using damp hands, perform a few sets of folds: Imagine the dough in the bowl has four sides. Grab the dough on one side, stretch it up 8 to 10 inches (20 to 25 cm), and lay it across the dough below. Repeat with the next side until you've gone around the dough a few times and it's well mixed. Each time you fold all 4 sides is considered one set. Flip the dough over, cover it again, and set a timer for 15 minutes.

3. Perform one set of folds and flip the dough. Cover and set aside, setting a timer for 30 minutes.

4. Perform another set of folds and flip the dough. Cover and set aside, setting a timer for 30 minutes.

5. Perform another set of folds and flip the dough. Cover and set aside, setting a timer for 30 minutes.

6. Perform the last set of folds, then spread the remaining 1 tablespoon olive oil on the bottom of a 9 × 13-inch (23 × 33 cm) pan, then place the dough folds side down in the pan, shaping and stretching it into a rectangle in the center of the pan. Cover the top of the dough with 1 or 2 teaspoons of olive oil using your hands. Set aside in a warm place, such as an oven with the light on or an oven set to proof. Set a timer for 1 hour.

7. To prepare the toppings: Place a tomato on a cutting board and slice it in half lengthwise. Cut each half at an angle into two even pieces (going from 10 o'clock to 4 o'clock). Flip one side of the angled tomato and place it together with the other side to form a perfect heart shape. Repeat this process with all the tomatoes.

8. Once the 1-hour timer goes off, the dough should be fluffy, bubbly, and doubled in size. Stretch it to fill the pan from corner to corner and use your fingers to poke holes in it all over.
9. Preheat the oven to 425°F (220° C).
10. Decorate the focaccia with tomato hearts, cheese, and rosemary leaves, then sprinkle the dough with flake salt or coarse salt.
11. Bake for 15 to 20 minutes, until golden brown on top. Remove from the oven and transfer to a wire rack to cool. Enjoy warm!

TIPS

For more patties, simply double the recipe. For the potatoes, I recommend getting the largest heart-shaped cookie cutter you can find to make as many large fry hearts as possible. I used a 1½- to 2-inch (4 to 5 cm) cookie cutter. You can use two similar-size cutters. Save the potato scraps to make mashed potatoes or hashbrowns later.

LOVE BITES

TOTAL TIME: 45 MINUTES **YIELD:** 2 SERVINGS

Prepare to win over the heart of your main squeeze with this adorable heart-themed burger and fries!

FOR THE BURGERS

2 hamburger buns
2 whole leaves lettuce
2 large slices cheddar cheese
2 large slices tomato
8 slices thick-cut bacon
2 beef patties

FOR THE OVEN FRIES

1 tablespoon olive oil, plus more for greasing
4 large russet potatoes, washed and peeled
¼ teaspoon salt, plus more for salting the water
1 teaspoon garlic powder
1 teaspoon dried parsley
½ teaspoon dried rosemary
Dash of black pepper

1. To make the burgers: Using a 4-inch (10 cm) heart-shaped cookie cutter, press down through the top and bottom of each bun. Using a 3-inch (7.5 cm) heart-shaped cookie cutter, cut hearts out of the lettuce and cheese slices. Using a 2-inch (5 cm) heart-shaped cookie cutter, cut hearts from tomato slices. Set aside.

2. To make the fries: Preheat the oven to 400°F (205°C). Line a baking sheet with parchment paper and spray with cooking spray or brush with oil. Slice the potatoes into ¼-inch-thick (6 mm) slices. Using heart-shaped metal cookie cutters, cut out as large and as many hearts as you can from each slice, setting the scraps aside. Bring a large saucepan half-filled with salted water to boil over high heat, then add the potatoes. Reduce the heat and simmer potatoes for about 3 minutes. Drain the potatoes thoroughly and let cool.

3. Place the potato hearts in a bowl and toss with the olive oil, garlic powder, parsley, rosemary, salt, and pepper. Spread them on a rimmed baking sheet and roast them for 25 to 30 minutes, until crispy and golden brown, flipping the potatoes and rotating the pan halfway through.

4. As the potatoes are roasting, prepare your bacon: Lay the slices of bacon on a pan over medium-high heat. Flip once the bottoms begin to brown, about 4 minutes, cooking until firm for about another 4 minutes. Lay the bacon on a paper towel–lined plate to soak up the extra grease. Once cooled enough to handle, use the metal heart-shaped cookie cutter to cut the bacon into hearts. Set aside.

5. Using the 4-inch (10 cm) cookie cutter or a knife, create heart shapes from the burger patties. Cook the beef patties in a medium-sized skillet over medium-high heat, flipping once, for 8 to 12 minutes, until they reach 165°F (74°C). Remove from the heat. Top each burger with a cheese heart, allowing it to melt slightly. Place a bun bottom on each plate, followed by heart-shaped lettuce, burger with cheese, tomato, and bun top. Surround with heart fries, 3 pieces of heart-shaped bacon, and your favorite condiments.

PROSECCO COCKTAIL

TOTAL TIME: 10 MINUTES **YIELD:** 2 SERVINGS

Looking for a bubbly Valentine's Day love potion to sweeten up your sweethearts? Look no further, because this cocktail is love at first sip! With prosecco, elderflower liqueur, and sweet strawberry puree, topped with a cute heart-shaped strawberry, this recipe is the perfect love-filled-libation for celebrating romance or friendship.

2 cups (300 g) halved strawberries with stem removed, plus 2 medium strawberries, for garnish
2 tablespoons honey, melted
4 tablespoons (60 ml) elderflower liqueur
1/2 cup (120 ml) prosecco

1. In a blender, add the halved strawberries, melted honey, and 1 to 2 tablespoons of water and blend until pureed.
2. In a cocktail shaker over ice, pour in the elderflower liqueur and ½ cup (120 ml) strawberry puree and shake well until chilled. Strain into two glasses over ice, and top with the prosecco.
3. Cut out a v in the top center of the remaining strawberries, removing the stems, to create the heart shape, then use a cocktail pick to perch each on the top of each glass.
4. Serve and enjoy!

TIPS

To make a pitcher batch, simply quadruple the recipe and strain into a pitcher. Use 4 cups (600 g) halved strawberries, ¼ cup (60 ml) melted honey, ½ cup (120 ml) elderflower liqueur, and 1 cup (240 ml) prosecco. You can make the strawberry hearts the day before, and store them in a paper towel–lined sealed container in the fridge for use in the cocktail.

SOMETIMES YOU MISS A SEASON

Life in this era in history is busy, and there are so many ways that we can end up feeling like we aren't keeping up, which is sad because life doesn't need to be led in a constant state of busyness. We all have moments where there's just not enough time. That said, I would hate for this book to make it seem like every single year I create all these scenes and all these setups for every single holiday. That's just not how life is!

Some years I put on and host a magnificent Mother's Day but opt for a low-key Father's Day. Other years, Mother's Day passes with no more than a dinner at a favorite local restaurant, but then a spring family games night on a rainy day later takes center stage, above any holiday!

My wish is that the inspiration within these pages finds you where you are at, bringing you inspiration and ideas to get creative and celebrate the season with your favorite people, whenever it fits, however it looks, from year to year.

After all, life isn't made up of one year of seasons and occasions. It's a mosaic of quirky small traditions as well as the over-the-top and lavish ones, each holding special places in our hearts for reasons big and small.

No matter what that looks like, take those pictures, keep those memories.

INDEX

P

Q

R

S

T

V

W

Z

SPECIAL THANKS

I could not have created this book without the love and support of my wonderful husband, Dan, and the inspiration given to me by my little muses, my children, Lila and Cade. They are my favorite people ever to gather with. They are always cheering me on and humoring me in all my ideas and adventures in the kitchen and gardens, despite the chaos my creativity sometimes leaves in its wake. They make every moment wild and wondrous, and I could not be luckier to have them as my people.

To my mom and dad, who are no longer with us, thank you for instilling in me my most cherished passions—gardening, food, family—and for always cheering me on in every endeavor. I truly believe that the reason that I think work is fun is because of the two of you.

To all the wonderful friends I've made online, many of whom I've never met in person but truly hope I do one day, thank you for being a part of my incredible social media community of kindred spirits, for all the inspiring ways you share, and for motivating me to keep sharing.

And to the rest of my family and friends, what would be the point and where would be the joy in all this effort if it weren't for this incredible circle I get to share it with?!

You make it all worthwhile. Thank you.

ABOUT THE AUTHOR

Robyn Chubey began blending her expertise as a professional photographer in 2018 with her passion for seasonal living, following her move to Prairie Glow Acres, a picturesque farm in East St. Paul, Manitoba, Canada. Since then, she has used her creative talents to capture and share the beauty of home and garden life.

Through her social media channels, @life_of_glow, Robyn showcases a wide array of DIY projects, recipes, and gardening tips. She also connects with her local community by hosting workshops, garden tours, and other engaging events.

Combining a lifetime of gardening experience with her love for teaching, Robyn inspires others to embrace the changing seasons through food, decor, and crafts, encouraging intentional and sustainable living in harmony with nature.

First published in 2026 by Rock Point, an imprint of The Quarto Group,
135 West 36th Street, 13th Floor, New York, NY 10018, USA
(212) 779-4972 www.Quarto.com

EEA Representation, WTS Tax d.o.o.,
Žanova ulica 3, 4000 Kranj, Slovenia.
www.wts-tax.si

Rock Point titles are also available at discount for retail, wholesale, promotional, and bulk purchase. For details, contact the Special Sales Manager by email at specialsales@quarto.com or by mail at The Quarto Group, Attn: Special Sales Manager, 100 Cummings Center Suite 265D, Beverly, MA 01915 USA.

10 9 8 7 6 5 4 3 2 1

ISBN: 978-1-57715-532-4

Digital edition published in 2026
eISBN: 978-0-7603-9661-2

Library of Congress Cataloging-in-Publication Data

Names: Chubey, Robyn author
Title: Gather together : delightful décor and simple recipes for every occasion / Robyn Chubey.
Description: New York, NY, USA : Rock Point, an imprint of The Quarto Group, 2026. Includes index. | Summary: "Take the stress out of entertaining with Gather Together, a unique collection of easy DIY décor projects and simple, delicious recipes"— Provided by publisher.
Identifiers: LCCN 2025017815 (print) | LCCN 2025017816 (ebook) | ISBN 9781577155324 | ISBN 9780760396612 ebook
Subjects: LCSH: Seasonal cooking | Table setting and decoration | Entertaining | LCGFT: Cookbook
Classification: LCC TX714 .C4959 2026 (print) | LCC TX714 (ebook) | DDC 641.5/64--dc23/eng/20250702
LC record available at https://lccn.loc.gov/2025017815
LC ebook record available at https://lccn.loc.gov/2025017816

Group Publisher: Rage Kindelsperger
Creative Director: Laura Drew
Managing Editor: Cara Donaldson
Senior Acquiring Editor: Nicole James
Editor: Keyla Pizarro-Hernández
Cover Design: Marisa Kwek
Interior Design: Verso Design

Printed in Huizhou City, Guangdong, China TT122025